AS I REMEMBER

A Walk Through My Years
at Hughes Aircraft 1961–1997

Scott Walker

ISBN 978-0-9841456-7-6

Photos in this book are largely from the collection of Scott Walker. Some photos were available from GFDI conventions through massive multi-author collaboration sites. These include:

Two photos of the Phoenix missile on an F-14 aircraft
Photo of the IIR Maverick
Photo of an A-10 firing a Maverick
Discovery Science Center, Santa Ana, CA
Chiang Kai Shek memorial in Taiwan

The cover photo of the author from the *Fortune* magazine article (1/27/1992) is by photographer Blake Little, used with permission.

Hawthorne Publishing
15601 Oak Road
Carmel
IN 46033 (317) 867-5183
www.hawthornepub.com

Printed and bound in the United States of America

I'm only passing through on my way to somewhere...
Are you going to somewhere, too?

Cassie Walker

CONTENTS

PREFACE

This account of my career at Hughes Aircraft was intended primarily for my descendants. I would like for them to know more about my life's work. Some of my contemporaries may also find portions of the story of interest, at least I hope so. Hughes Aircraft Company (later to become GM Hughes Electronics) is simply the stage for the play. This is not a definitive history of Hughes Aircraft, a story yet to be written; nevertheless, as some aspects of its illustrative history are revealed as my story unfolds, some members of the general public with curiosity about Hughes Aircraft may be interested in this book. For readers who are unfamiliar with the company, a short overview of the company's formation is also provided.

The title of this book is quite deliberate. The events are as true "as I remember." If some readers have knowledge regarding various happenings, they will undoubtedly recall some details differently. I suspect my errors are of little consequence. Also, since I am writing strictly from memory, I caution against using the histories and stories in this report as accurate reference sources.

Some of my colleagues in this report are identified by name and some only by position. Either way, they are all friends. Almost all the successes at Hughes are due to the combined work of many highly skilled and industrious people. If on occasion I used "I" when I should have said "we," or I used "we" when I should have said "they," I ask the reader's tolerance for a hubristic pride in our company.

The projects and technologies in this report are at least once removed from today's era. For example, the award of the Navy's Phoenix missile celebrated in the first chapter subsequently went through full engineering development, was put into service, and is now phased out of the inventory. By the way, the Phoenix was fired in anger only once, during an incident in Libya.

Similarly, my comments and observations in the last chapter are meant for the period fifteen years ago when I was dealing with GM. The post-bankruptcy General Motors of 2010 is not the same company.

Although I have described a little of my early years, this book really begins with the period in which my wife and I arrived in southern California for me to take a position at Hughes Aircraft, the only job I've had since college.

Happy reading.

INTRODUCTION

I was born in Brookville, Pennsylvania, on March 16, 1935. My dad, Dr. Gale H. Walker, delivered me. With the Depression at its worst, Dad soon tired of being paid in kind—a cord of wood, for example, instead of cash—for medical care. So the family moved to Polk, Pennsylvania, where he took a state appointment as a doctor at Polk State School, an institution for mentally deficient children. Dad became superintendent of Polk State School and made several nationally recognized contributions in his chosen field, serving a term as president of the American Association on Mental Deficiency, and was known for his nationwide study on standards for institutions related to mental deficiency. The small hospital at Polk was named after him, and he was also recognized for his contribution to the development of the Salk polio vaccine when it came time for the very first trials on children.

When my parents divorced in 1944, I moved to McKeesport, near Pittsburgh, with my mother and my brother, Ted, to live with Grandpa and Grandma Scott. Their surname, Scott, is my middle name. I had been named William, after my granddad Dr. William J. Walker, who practiced medicine in Homestead, Pennsylvania.

Grandpa Scott worked for U.S. Steel for forty-five years. After he reached retirement age in February 1945, he was asked to stay on until the war was over. After retirement he chose a warmer climate, so in October of that year, my mother, brother, and I, age ten, joined Grandpa and Grandma Scott in moving to Statesville, North Carolina, a small town fifty miles from Charlotte (my wife Cassie's hometown). My grandparents lived out a nice retirement in Statesville, with Grandma passing on in 1969 and Grandpa three years later at the age of 92. Grandpa Scott was like a surrogate father to me.

I grew up in Statesville, was an Eagle Scott, and enjoyed playing trombone and piano. My senior year, I gave a solo piano recital at the local college, white dinner jacket and all. The summer before my senior year in high school, I met Cassie at a Baptist summer camp at Fort Caswell on the Atlantic coast. At the time she was one year older than I, but somehow I am now a year older than she, and look it. We dated my entire senior year (I drove to Charlotte almost every weekend in my World War II jeep) and continued to date while I was in college.

I seriously considered going to music school and envisioned myself becoming a conductor, but ended up going to Wake Forest College (now Wake Forest University) with the intention of graduating with a degree in business administration. However, during my first semester, I soon realized the business math being taught was not challenging enough to interest me and dropped business administration as my college major.

Fortunately, while I was a college freshman, quartered in the home of a professor whose brilliant son, Jasper, was only 17 and already a sophomore at Wake Forest, I discovered he was majoring in physics. Talking with Jasper while playing chess and learning he played a much better game than I, I decided to change my major to physics. Although I had yet to take a course in physics, including in high school, I decided to go for a doctorate in that discipline. Why not? After all, I was from a line of doctors, albeit doctors of medicine. So first I earned a BS in physics from Wake Forest in 1957, an MA in physics at the University of Virginia in 1959, and finally a Ph.D. in physics at Virginia in 1961.

I went to the University of Virginia for graduate studies as a DuPont scholar for the first two years, then under a National Science Foundation scholarship for the last two years, with full tuition and living expenses paid for the four years.

In 1958, one year into my graduate studies, Cassie and I were married in the chapel at Wake Forest University in Winston-Salem. We had been dating six years by that time and Cassie was head of the art department of a publishing company in Charlotte. After marrying and moving to Charlottesville, Virginia with me, she continued doing layouts and art work under subcontract and as an independent artist.

For my master's degree thesis I measured the lifetimes of positrons in the water/ice transition. My Ph.D. in nuclear physics involved the use of a Van de Graaff generator to measure the angular distribution of neutron backscattering for heavy nuclei to support the verification of the "optical model" of the nucleus.

After receiving my master's degree in 1959, I accepted a summer job at the Los Alamos Scientific Laboratory in New Mexico. Our summer in New Mexico played an important role in our lives, because Cassie and I began to envision living west of the Mississippi. I had grown up on the east coast mostly thinking of the United States in terms of north and south, not east and west, but now we were attracted to America's beautiful west.

Then, in the spring of 1961, I found myself in Washington, DC at a meeting of the American Physical Society. After giving a short paper on my terribly exciting measurements of neutron scattering from heavy nuclei, I was sitting in the hotel lobby smoking my curved pipe when I came to a rather belated realization. I liked physics but liked something else more. That something more was rather unclear at the time but turned out to be complex, multidisciplinary interactions in the industrial world. After eight years pursuing my goal to be a physicist, I realized I didn't think like a typical physicist. That realization brought a fortunate end to a potential career in physics at a university.

Thanks in large part to our summer in New Mexico, I interviewed for a position at the Sandia Corporation in Albuquerque. In spite of an excellent offer from Sandia, I remember commenting, "I wonder where we would want to go for our first vacation? I bet it would be California. And, if we like California enough to choose it first for a vacation, why not just live there?" So I interviewed at Hughes Aircraft and at North American Rockwell in southern California. I chose Hughes by a large margin.

At age 26, then, I had graduated with a Ph.D. in physics, and now, in June 1961, Cassie and I headed off to California and Hughes Aircraft Company and the only job I would ever have.

CHAPTER ONE: 1961–1975

MISSILE SYSTEMS

THE EARLY YEARS

GETTING STARTED

After driving across the country in Cassie's robin's-egg-blue 1954 Buick Roadmaster convertible, this young married couple arrived in California in late June 1961. By the time we got to San Bernardino, we started looking for movie stars. When we got off the freeway in Hollywood, I did a U-turn at a street corner where it wasn't allowed and immediately got my first-ever traffic ticket, ten minutes after arriving in Los Angeles.

We spent several nights at the Miramar Hotel in Santa Monica while looking for an apartment by the ocean, driving from Malibu to Long Beach and finding to our surprise how little was available near the water. But we finally found the perfect apartment just being completed on the Esplanade in Redondo Beach. Gosh! They wanted $210 per month. That was more than I could imagine. After a lunch out on the Redondo Pier with a tearful Cassie, who truly knew better than I what a good value was, I gave in. I'm glad I did, but I sure wasn't going to tell the folks back east just how much we were paying.

I went in to Hughes a day before the two-day Fourth of July break just to say hello, expecting to start work the first day after the holiday. "Start right now and get paid for the holiday," the human resources manager told me. It didn't seem right, but it sure was OK with me. We went to Beverly Hills to buy shoes. I think I had only sandals, and Cassie was almost barefoot.

My starting salary was $221 per week, and I couldn't believe how much money that was. Since the banks were still providing large silver dollars upon request, I would cash my weekly paycheck and ask for it in silver dollars. I would search through the coins for dates and often carry the rest around in a large sack when shopping. Several months later, the banks stopped providing silver dollars, but by then I had collected maybe sixty dates. I still have the collection, which I'm sure is worth more than sixty dollars today.

I've talked about my name before, but there is more to it than that. I had grown up being call Bill Walker. However, at the University of Virginia, there was another Bill Walker in the physics department, one year older than I, so everyone started calling me Bill Jr. I didn't like that and asked people to call me by my middle name, Scott, the last name of my maternal grandparents. Since I was quite close to them it seemed right to me. Upon graduation, I rather expected to go back to being called Bill.

Now I had to think about this. In the spring of 1961, I had flown out to LA for interviews with Hughes Aircraft and North American Aviation. When I started to work at Hughes that summer, I couldn't recall whether I had interviewed as Scott or Bill. Apparently I had interviewed as Scott, because they gave me a plaque for my desk that said "Scott Walker." Because of that plaque, I am called Scott to this day. However, in North Carolina, Cassie's family still called her Doris, her actual first name, and my family still called me Bill. So the joke was Doris and Bill left North Carolina, went to California, and changed their names to Cassie and Scott. To this day, back east we are still Doris and Bill.

EARLY ASSIGNMENTS

I knew very little about system analysis, radar, infrared sensors, or guided missiles, the stuff Hughes Aircraft dealt with. During the first week on the job they sort of forgot about me and put me in someone's office while the person was on vacation. I started reading the fellow's literature. It wasn't long before I was trying to figure out how Falcon missiles for air-to-air combat worked. I learned this Falcon missile used proportional guidance, whatever that was. It seemed to me that proportional guidance would always result in tail pursuit for the missile when homing in on an enemy airplane, which is exactly wrong.

Since no one was giving me an assignment, I wandered down the hall to a section head manager, Paul Kennard, and struck up a conversation. Paul's dad was the author of one of my favorite college physics books, which really impressed me. "It seems to me proportional guidance always ends up in a tail pursuit trajectory," I said, having misunderstood it completely. He kindly tried to explain the subject to me before he realized I didn't know Falcon missiles had been in production for ten years. Finally, he said, "Scott, let's put it this way: we have already manufactured 30,000 Falcon proportional-guidance missiles." Oh.

On Friday I finally knocked on the department manager's door and complained that I wasn't usefully employed. He assigned me to a brilliant section head, Milt Radant, who mostly to keep me busy, asked me to calculate the range at which a friendly airplane radar could burn-through the jammer on an hypothetical enemy aircraft. Hmm, all right. So the whole next week I laboriously started figuring out radar transmissions, target cross-sections, antenna gains, atmospheric attention, etc., inventing what must be happening, using equivalents from my experience with neutron scattering measurements I had done in my graduate study.

At the end of the following week, I showed Milt my calculation. He scribbled a calculation on a piece of paper and thirty seconds later said, "Yes, that's right." I asked, "What did you do?" He just used a radar range equation that I had never heard of and had just spent days re-inventing. He said, "Go to the library and start reading the MIT radiation lab books." The Rad Lab reference books recorded the radar work done at the Massachusetts Institute of Technology during World War II. Boy, what a treasure. I didn't even know we had a library. I got my radar education from the Rad Lab series. Volume 13 was particularly useful for me by showing how to do look-down ground clutter calculations. Before long I became the lead guy to do ground clutter calculations and even proposed new research on the subject.

A week or so later they had me working on a counter-measure calculation for a new type of enemy jammer. I wrote a short memo with some simple calculations. Since my clearance was still only at the Confidential level and my memo was classified Secret, I wasn't supposed to read my own memo.

PHOENIX MISSILE

In the fall of 1961, Milt Radant and I were put on the proposal team for the Phoenix Missile System, which included a missile, radar, and a fire control system for a new Navy aircraft. The Phoenix System would provide a major new defense for our aircraft carriers.

If we won the contract, it would be our first missile manufactured for the Navy. The specifications were difficult, requiring a long-range, 50-mile missile that could be launched in salvos of up to six at a time. All six missiles were to hit six incoming enemy aircraft that had the nasty objective of sinking our aircraft carrier. The long-range missiles had a mid-course phase to receive directional updates from the launch aircraft until the missiles switched over to their own radar seekers. A critical question was: Should the mid-course phase be a command-inertial guidance system to give updates on enemy aircraft maneuvers, or should the mid-course involve the launch aircraft's radar providing time-shared bursts of information (what we called semi-active pulse Doppler mid-course)?

Although I was assigned to the pulse Doppler team, I believed the company would choose the command-inertial approach. After a day's work on the proposal, I would come home complaining to Cassie at our oceanfront apartment in Redondo Beach. I believed I was only helping to write an appendix for what was not going to be used.

Well, we won the Phoenix program. That in itself was enough to celebrate. But for me at least, equally important, our pulse Doppler approach was chosen over command-inertial mid-course guidance. By the time I got home the day we won, I had several sheets in the wind. I got out my trombone, went out on our front porch by the ocean, and serenaded the neighbors in celebration. Ever since then, whenever I play my trombone, our friends ask if we won another missile program.

I was given the option of either joining the Phoenix program team or staying on in advanced system studies. I took a long walk around the Culver City plant, trying to see into the future, and came back to the lab manager, Harvey Palmer, to say, "I want to stay in advanced systems." That was one of the little decisions that shape so much of a person's future.

By then we had been living in California about a year. How did we feel about the decision we had made to move west to live? Well, we liked both our decision and the state itself. There was a saying: "If you want to know what life will be like in ten years, go to California." That is how we felt. On the negative side, I went through some home-sickness for my family back east. However, once we took a two weeks' vacation back to North Carolina after the first year, I appreciated that the east coast was really only a day away by plane. Outgrowing home-sickness isn't unusual, and we did that.

Perhaps more surprising, though, was one thing about California which really bothered me, a factor that wasn't unique to California.

That was the lack of respect for your word as signature. I guess my years at both Wake Forest College and the University of Virginia had influenced my thinking. At Thomas Jefferson's University of Virginia a student signed his or her test, and when that happened, that signature was the honor pledge that that student had not cheated. It was considered an affront for the professor to stay in the classroom while students were taking a test because that implied a supervisor needed to be there to catch cheating. Well, in California when I wrote a check at a store in that age before credit cards, the clerk asked for my identification. I was really bothered by that. "You mean you don't accept my signature?" Of course over time, I learned to accept that the clerk was only doing what he or she was told. It was not a matter of not trusting me. Still today, however, I consider a man or woman's signature represents that person's word of honor.

LASERS

It was 1960, I believe, when Hughes Aircraft's research laboratory in Malibu made the world's first optical laser, the ruby laser. The company was quite proud of this achievement, and now the entire industry was abuzz as to what applications could come from it all. In 1962 Pat Hyland, the company's general manager, was concerned that Hughes was falling behind on applications in spite of being the first to achieve laser action. He asked our advanced systems laboratory to do a study of what should be done. Since I had elected to stay on in advanced systems rather than going with the Phoenix program, I was available and was asked to do a study.

Except for maybe reading about them in *Scientific American* magazine, I knew almost nothing about lasers. My first trip out of the plant after being there a year was to go to the University of California, Los Angeles (UCLA) to read about lasers in their library. Walking around the UCLA campus, I noticed a poster looking for activists who were willing to go to Alabama and march in support of civil rights. The poster said you would be arrested but should get out of jail in time for the fall semester. This was a whole different world for me. The world itself was changing.

I wrote a long essay. The first half concerned what a laser was and how it worked. The second half of the report was on various possible applications. One application that was continually being batted around in those days was using lasers as weapons to blow up enemy airplanes. I added up the unknowns, such as how much energy it would take to destroy the target, and what was the target's absorption versus reflection coefficients; discussed uncertainties in the ability to point the narrow laser beam, homed in on variations in atmospheric attention, along with the unknown power levels that could be obtained; and analyzed the laser's efficiencies. I came to the conclusion that laser weapons were indeed practical but with the slight uncertainty of about 10 to the 12th power! As the years have rolled by, I read about new breakthroughs and noted they may have eliminated yet another of my 12 powers of 10 uncertainties. I don't really know what is going on today, but I suspect now some 50 years later we might be getting down to just a couple of powers of 10 from a truly practical weapon. Maybe we are even there under very special conditions.

MY FIRST PROMOTION

I was heading for advancement at Hughes, but it seemed a little ironic to me. My first encounter with Hughes Aircraft had been in January 1961, when I went to the American Physical Society meeting in New York with the explicit objective of finding a job when I completed my doctoral degree the following June. Cassie was with me along with Van Hudson, my research partner, who was on the same mission. Van found a job at the Lawrence Radiation Laboratory in Livermore, California, working on nuclear bombs. Well, I knew nothing more to say when being interviewed by Hughes than, "Are you doing anything in neutron physics?"

A month or so later I got a phone call from a Hughes department head asking if I would like a job in system analysis. I didn't know what system analysis was. He explained it to me, and I responded that it seemed that they were looking for an electrical engineer but couldn't find one. "Oh, no, we want physicists also," he was quick to tell me.

Well, I took the job at Hughes as a "member of the technical staff." Now here I was two years later, and Hughes wanted to promote me to "staff engineer." "I thought we had discussed this earlier," I argued. "I'm not an engineer; I'm a physicist, and furthermore I was suspicious all along that you didn't want physicists. If you can't call a physicist a physicist maybe I should leave Hughes."

Harvey Palmer, my laboratory manager, asked to meet this guy who wouldn't take his promotion. I explained it all. The net result was they created the position "staff physicist" and then followed up with "staff mathematician" and other similar titles.

AIR-TO-SURFACE MISSILES
AN AGING PRODUCT LINE

Hughes Aircraft had become strategic to the defense of the country because they developed the Falcon missiles. During the period leading up to the Cold War, the Falcon could effectively take out incoming Russian bombers carrying nuclear bombs. As a result the company grew rapidly, going from around 3,000 employees in 1950 to over 30,000 by 1958. However, the primary threat then changed from nuclear bombers to nuclear ballistic missiles. As a result, in 1958 the Air Force cancelled the next-generation interceptors and the next generation of Falcon missiles, putting our company in an awkward position. We were looking at a serious decline in revenue.

Fortunately, under the leadership of Pat Hyland, the company successfully diversified into other military electronics and space systems. We invented our future. We were the first to develop synchronous satellites for communication. We built the Surveyor, the first vehicle to soft land on the moon. We had the first optical laser, and so forth. Eventually Hughes would become the world's largest military electronics supplier.

But when I joined the company in 1961, I had no idea I was part of a phase of rebounding from the decline of the Falcon missile business. One telltale measure, however, was where I would park my car. Never an early arriver, at first I could still park by the side entrance near my office. As the company started to grow again, I found I had to find parking off-site and walk in. Despite the award of the Phoenix missile system, I began to question the continued vitality of the market for air-to-air missiles in a climate where our satellite division was growing rapidly. Even the department head who hired me left Hughes to work on space programs at North American. Things might not be rebounding as well as they should have been.

I heard an inspiring talk by the division manager of our space programs and darn near went up to him afterwards to introduce myself. If I had, I'm sure he would have invited me into his operations, and the rest of my career at Hughes would have been entirely different. Instead, I stayed in the aeronautical systems organization, and things did go forward at Hughes. It was just one of those major forks in the road of life that are often not recognized at the time.

A NEW PRODUCT LINE

The state of the art of conventional bombing left a major need for far better bombing accuracy. There were several efforts in the military to develop effective guided air-to-surface missiles, but the tactical Air Force and Navy were still forced to rely mostly on conventional bombing with accuracies ranging in hundreds of feet at best.

Recognizing a market need, Hughes Aircraft invested in air-to-surface missile technology. Ted Wong and Ken Friedenthal formed a new department to develop products for this market. I joined the department and never again worked on air-to-air missiles. The principal problem was how to specify ground targets and find a means to guide missiles to them. Guidance technology was akin to physics and close to my technical comfort zone. Before long I was promoted to senior staff physicist in the air-to-surface missiles department, and as the activities increased, I became section head for advanced guidance. For the next ten years, I worked exclusively on advanced air-to-surface missiles.

OPTICAL CORRELATION GUIDANCE

One air-launch requirement that was far out in 1964 was for a "hitting missile" that could be launched from over the horizon and hit a specified target within a certain number of feet. Today, we can do that routinely with GPS guidance, something that didn't exist then.

The Air Force at Wright-Patterson Air Force Base in Dayton, Ohio, sent out a request for proposals to study guidance systems for this "hitting missile." I was the proposal manager for our response, which we called the "Target Homing Missile System." We won the study by proposing optical correlation guidance that used an image of the target stored in the missile. After an inertial mid-course guidance phase, an onboard television camera would match an image of the terrain with the stored photograph to precisely locate the intended target.

Little did I know the Air Force expected to award the study to another company, which apparently had already done the behind-the-scenes work setting up the program. Quite possibly General Schriver, the four-star Air Force general and commander of the entire Air Force Systems Command, had expected the other company to do the study. Anyway, General Schriver called Pat Hyland, general manager at Hughes, asking to come to Culver City and get briefed on our program.

My Air Force project director at Wright Pat called me to say that the general would be coming to pay me a visit. I noted it but didn't think much more about it, thinking he would just drop into the office, which I shared with another engineer, and we would talk awhile. I never bothered to mention it to my department head, let alone tell Pat Hyland, the head of the company. It took corporate headquarters several days to find out just who at Hughes had this small program the general wanted a briefing on. When they located me, the headquarters staff was all excited. They said, "What do you want? Name it." Being a fast student, I said, "Well… paint my optical lab and get me a new optical bench." I also asked for some other equipment I wanted.

When the general came on a Monday, higher-ups in our company did all the glad-handing stuff. Finally I got to lead them to my lab for show and tell, only to forget how to go from the corporate briefing room to my optical lab. So here was a four-star general and I walking along and talking with a long trail of Hughes executives and military support people behind us as I wandered around several corridors before finally finding my lab.

Over the next several years, we built an optical correlation seeker. We started field tests in New Mexico using a helicopter to simulate the final terminal dive. I wanted the helicopter to simulate a near-vertical descent on the target while the optical map-matching correlation was being recorded. The pilots didn't like my idea of auto-rotating down to simulate the terminal trajectory, so I was forced to compromise a little. Yet the helicopter flight test program kept dragging along, and I didn't know why. Finally someone let me know the tests probably wouldn't be completed until the ski season in New Mexico was over. My lead guy there was skiing every weekend and was in no hurry to come home. Well, I fixed that.

In the end, however, for a number of reasons, the optical correlation approach didn't pan out.

CANOGA PARK

As the revitalized company started to grow rapidly in the 1960s, Hughes was forced to expand from the Culver City facility, where the old Flying Boat had been built, to other southern California locations. Hughes purchased a plant in Newport Beach for semiconductors and a one-hundred-acre site in Fullerton, also in Orange County. A number of high-rise buildings were established around the Los Angeles airport. A beautiful facility in Canoga Park at the west end of the San Fernando Valley, built by Ramo/Woolridge (the R and W of TRW Inc.), was purchased by Hughes in 1965. The question was what operations would be moved to Canoga Park. It seemed the various senior managers all wanted to stay in Culver City near the corporate offices and probably much nearer to their homes. When asked, they came up with ideas such as putting the library, human resources, warehousing, and so forth out in Canoga Park. The president, John Richardson, finally had enough of this chatter and on his own formed a new stand-alone division for missiles, while space programs, fire control systems, radar, infrared, and other electronic systems remained in Culver City.

In 1964 Cassie, our first son Tyler, and I had moved from our apartment in Redondo Beach, 15 miles south of Culver City, to a new home way out in the west San Fernando Valley, 30 miles north of Culver City and, by sheer coincidence, one mile from what would become the new Hughes facility at Canoga Park. So we were well placed for the move. And now the company was sorting out who would join this new missile division there.

At the time my optical correlation work, located in Culver City, had potential application not only to missile guidance but also as a means of updating airplane inertial navigation systems. My lab manager, who planned to stay in Culver City, dropped by my office to ask, "Scott, where do you think optical correlation is going to be best used: missile guidance or airplane navigation update?" He made no reference to Culver City or Canoga Park, but that was in his mind.

I said, "I believe optical correlation has its best chances in missile guidance." He assumed I would know that taking that stance meant I would not be staying in Culver City along with most of the heavy hitters and insiders. I followed with the comment, "I live a mile from the plant." Without saying a word, he just smiled and walked out of my office. With that, I went to Canoga Park.

When we bought our home in Canoga Park I didn't know the facility was there and certainly didn't know Hughes Aircraft was going to purchase the place a year later. When the freeways were wide open, the drive from Canoga Park to the Culver City plant was 30 minutes, but we soon discovered that the freeways are never wide open during work days; Friday evenings were more like 90 minutes getting home. And now, it would be only five minutes between office and home.

When we moved into our three-bedroom home, Tyler was one year old. In 1966 our second son, Morgan, was born, and in 1969 Brandon joined us, rounding out our family. We lived in Canoga Park until 1973.

MISSILE SYSTEMS DIVISION

When the Missile Systems Division in Canoga Park was formed in 1965, I was promoted to department head in the Advanced Projects Organization. They gave me the privilege to name my department. When I chose "Conceptual Design Department," someone commented that was a good name for my way of working. I doubt the name was ever used before or since at Hughes.

Although I was involved with a number of seeker technologies, video guidance dominated our systems. In simple terms, the missile incorporated a small television camera in the nose. Before launch, the pilot or fire control officer on the airplane located the intended target in a cockpit display as viewed by the missile camera. The operator would lock a video gate around the target and launch the missile. The missile would continue to home in on the designated gated area with very high accuracy.

The Navy had one of the first successful television-guided weapons in the Walleye, intended for large targets such as bridges. Hughes became a second source for Walleye and eventually helped in the development of Walleye II with a larger warhead.

The first major win at the new Missile Systems Division was the Air Force's Maverick missile, which also used television guidance. The principal target was the tank. I had system responsibility for the seeker during the proposal phase. The Maverick required a more advanced tracker that tracked the centroid of the target rather than just an edge, as used by Walleye.

In 1968 I was promoted again, this time to product line manager for advanced air-to-surface missiles. I didn't exactly know what that entailed, but quickly learned to like it. I had the responsibility to deploy the division's discretionary funds for exploratory and advanced research for air-to-surface missiles and to win bids for related Air Force and Navy programs. The full-scale programs had their own resources to maintain their products.

To manage the advanced program funds I had a rather small group of perhaps ten or so engineers. One advantage of working with a small team was that we could conserve funds. Controlling funds gave you all the control you needed for the project. Of course, at times this made the large performing organizations unhappy with me because I would just conserve the funds when it wasn't an opportune time to disperse them.

As might be expected, when there were advanced project operations such as mine and full-scale program operations with somewhat overlapping charters, the question arose as to which team should get the funding and take the lead for new related developments. In my case, that mostly meant should my team control the funds for advanced versions, or should the much larger Maverick program office control them?

This thorny topic was featured at one of our annual off-site meetings. The Maverick program was to present their position first, and I was to give my retort as a follow-up. The night before the presentations, Jim Drake, the Maverick program manager, and I crawled under a dining table at the resort hotel with a bottle of spirits to sort it all out. We agreed to keep our powder dry and not entertain everyone with some form of a shoot-out. Once I knew our game plan, I was ready to go back to my room around 2 AM to prepare my Vu-Graphs for the next day's presentation.

When the division manager summed up the off-site meeting on Saturday morning, after we had made our presentations, he said, "Well, we still don't know how advanced systems and the program offices work together, but we do know Scott doesn't know how to spell." Guess the spirits interfered with the spelling on the Vu-Graphs I had made late that night. But the secret to the good relations between my advanced systems and the program office was simple: we just respected and liked each other.

ABORTED ADVANCED PROJECTS

Most exploratory developments do not make it into full-scale development, let alone go all the way to inventory. Still, these exploratory programs are good for both the military services and the participating companies. Let's recall several aborted projects.

A new type of missile seeker that employed laser designators was becoming popular. The laser might be airborne or in the hands of a ground observer. The operator would maintain the laser on the target; the missile or laser-guided bomb would then home in on the laser spot. Working with the Navy, I proposed the development of a dual-mode Walleye, which incorporated both a television and a laser seeker. The idea was to have both options available when the aircraft took off from an aircraft carrier. We had some success with the early development, but the concept never got the operational support needed for full-scale development and was terminated.

Another example: Responding to an Air Force request for a super-low-cost guided missile, my team worked up the design of a laser missile that incorporated the Zuni rocket as the basic vehicle. The enormous quantity of five-inch Zuni rockets in inventory brought us into the target range of $3K. It was an ugly-looking bird that turned out to be a real bummer of an idea. It pleased almost everyone at Hughes, including me, when the Air Force eventually dropped the project.

Another exploratory effort utilized a side-looking, synthetic-array radar. This very sophisticated all-weather, air-to-ground system was led by the radar systems team in Culver City and involved our Missile Division in Canoga Park. It was an exciting, revolutionary, stand-off, all-weather solution that just didn't make it into full development, probably due to its complexity.

An important program that did go into full development and inventory was the HARM, an advanced homing anti-radiation missile. Unfortunately, Texas Instruments won over our proposal. HARM replaced the outdated Shrike anti-radiation missile, which had been produced by TI. Perhaps it would have been too much to expect we could win; nevertheless, we gave it a good try and a win would have been a significant event for Hughes.

The final example of a hotly contested program that didn't exactly go my way started out as an idea for a small laser missile (six inches in diameter) for use in close air support. It was sponsored by Eglin Air Force Base at Fort Walton Beach, Florida. It seemed obvious to me that the requirement would best be met with a laser head on a 12-inch diameter Maverick missile and not a new six-inch missile. A Maverick derivative development would have been transferred to the Maverick program office at Wright-Patterson Air Force in Dayton, Ohio, whereas Eglin wanted to manage the development of a new six-inch missile in Florida. I proposed a Maverick derivative to Eglin anyway, knowing they didn't want it. I knew they would have to show the trade-offs of their six-inch missile against the Maverick and essentially had to award us a study contract, if only to counter the analysis behind our design.

The study became highly political, pitting Eglin's intended contractor's design against our design. I argued forcibly within the Air Force from high up in the Pentagon on down the hierarchy that Maverick was the right vehicle, but Eglin just wasn't going to buy in. I spent some sleepless nights tossing in bed on this one. I remember once walking down the middle of the street by our house around 2:30 in the morning, saying to myself, "Why can't the Air Force see that this should be a Maverick?"

Well, naturally, another company won the first phase to develop the laser seeker, not Hughes. And interestingly, they got into technical problems in the launch test phase. To shorten the story somewhat, eventually the program evolved into yet another competitor's laser seeker mounted on the Maverick, with Hughes completing the program and putting it into full production after all. I was right all along. We got a Maverick derivative; we just didn't get the laser seeker.

By the way, although my relation with a certain officer at Eglin during this difficult period was rather acrimonious, I continued to work on other programs there successfully. In fact, Eglin offered me a government GS-15 position, the highest grade available short of executive branch approval, which I turned down.

IMAGING INFRARED MAVERICK

If you were to ask me by what program I would like to be most remembered, I would say there are two. The IIR (imaging infrared) Maverick was the first of the two. (Much later in this book I will address the other.)

For me, at least, the IIR Maverick venture started during the Vietnam War with the need to better counter surface-to-air missiles (SAMs) that were downing our aircraft. One of my guys suggested an infrared hot-spot-seeking Maverick that would home in on the power generator associated with a SAM. My counterargument was that the hot power generator could be easily shielded, hiding the heat source. Or better yet, just set out a Hibachi pot away from the SAM, and our hot-spot seeker would home on that Hibachi. The program that did result from the requirement to counter the SAMs was the anti-radiation homing missile, HARM, mentioned in the last section.

Nevertheless, the exercise got us thinking about how to use infrared technology for Maverick to counter targets such as tanks at night. It was clear to me that the seeker must be able to distinguish small temperature differences and not just rely on tracking hot spots, such as the tank's engine. Sensors called FLIRs (forward-looking infrared) could locate a target within a cluttered background and were being used on aircraft. But FLIRs' sensors were large (bigger than a bread box) and rather expensive, costing well over $100K, while the total cost of the Maverick needed to be in the $20,000 to $40,000 range.

Accepting an imaging infrared seeker that would be good enough to be effective, small enough for a missile, and affordable was not easy. The general thinking in the industry and some parts of the military was to accept "pseudo-imaging" to reduce cost. Pseudo-imaging has poor imaging quality, but that quality is better than just a hot-spot seeker. My argument was that the nature of the requirement had nothing to do with cost. Quality imagery was needed first and foremost, and the closest to the real thing was the answer. Pseudo-imaging was simply not good enough. Somehow the costs had to be engineered down.

One significant cost-reduction idea our team came up with involved the scanner. A mechanical apparatus would scan the imagery across a linear array of IR detectors to generate the IR image. We proposed integrating 20 multifaceted scanning mirrors on the inside of the spinning free gyro needed for proportional guidance. Each mirror was offset in angle from the next. As the gyro spun around, it simultaneously performed the image scanning. I liked the term "free" gyro, as we got the image scanning for free.

The best way to achieve nighttime capability for Maverick was debated within the several interested companies and with the military for some time. Several proponents, including our Maverick program office, argued to use low-light television (LLTV) cameras. I contended LLTV still need some light, suffered blooming in bright light, and was poor at penetrating haze. I was steadfast within the company and with the military that the seeker must be IIR with good, clear imagery.

Eventually Wright-Patterson came to the same conclusion and put out a request for the advanced development program of an imaging infrared seeker for Maverick. This was a must win for us. They had $2 million, which they intended to divide between two contractors. Surely Hughes would win one of them, but I wanted it all.

Since we were able to show commercial applications, it was legal to buy-in on the contract. I asked the company for $1 million. Hughes president John Richardson gave me the money but said, "Make sure the Air Force appreciates we are spending it on their program." So for each dollar expended on the advanced development program, we only billed the Air Force 50 cents. This allowed us to build two seekers instead of just one, using $1 million from the government and $1 million from Hughes. No question we would win one of the two contracts.

However, I wanted the second million intended for another company. We came up with some goodies, starting with a program for a closed-cycle cryogenic engine instead of the nitrogen gas bottle otherwise required to cool the infrared detectors. The Air Force couldn't resist that. Well, that mopped up about $250K... $750K to go.

We came up with something pretty darn clever. On an F-4 fighter aircraft, Maverick missiles hang on a pylon as a cluster of three, with another cluster of three on the other wing. So instead of loading a total of six imaging infrared Mavericks on two pylons, we envisioned using one position to put a quality imager, almost as good as a full blown FLIR that would not be launched, on one of the six launch rails. Thus, an aircraft that otherwise did not have a FLIR could mount our Maverick FLIR and be much more effective in finding targets, handing off to a missile before launch. We offered to build a Maverick FLIR for $750K.

Well, that did it. Instead of getting one seeker from each of two contractors, the Air Force was getting from Hughes two seekers, a cryo-engine program, and an innovative Maverick FLIR, all for $2 million plus an additional $1 million Hughes investment. Goodbye to the other contractor. We had it sole source.

When we built our first seeker, I was still uncomfortable with image quality. I wanted it tested in a special way. I had our new infra-red imaging seeker mounted on a helicopter and took a ride at night through the harbor channel in San Diego. As the pilot flew toward a resort facility I was familiar with, I looked at the TV display of the seeker's imagery for particular structures I had in mind. (I seemed to re-member the resort had a dining table one could crawl under to discuss things.) I found it hard to locate familiar targets even without the dis-traction of encountering ground fire in a war zone. When I got back to Canoga Park, our technical director, who kept questioning my tenacity for quality imaging, asked what I thought after the night flight. I told him we were going to improve the imagery, not reduce it to save cost.

A favorite personal story related to IIR Maverick happened on a Saturday in the summer of 1974. We had recently purchased an his-toric Victorian home known as "Homewood" in La Cañada Flintridge near Pasadena. I was out in the backyard cutting the grass and started to think about the Maverick FLIR that was being flight tested. It had been flown back from the White Sands proving grounds in New Mexi-co for some repairs, and I had scheduled the Hughes Aero Commander to take it back to New Mexico Saturday for a test flight the following Monday.

I asked son Tyler if he wanted to go with me down to the Bur-bank airport to watch them load the Maverick FLIR on the Aero Commander. We drove down without mentioning it to Cassie. While watching them load the Maverick FLIR sensor on the airplane, I asked the Hughes pilot as to his flight plans. "Just flying down, dropping it off and flying back," was the reply. I asked if it was OK if Tyler and I went along. "Sure, it's your plane today," he said. So we climbed on-board for the 90-minute, one-way flight.

In flight to New Mexico, I started to think. On Monday night an F-4 airplane would locate a tank using the Maverick FLIR sensor, then transfer the lock-on to an adjacent IIR Maverick missile. No launches were planned, but this would be a world first: a FLIR lock-on followed by a transfer to an imaging infrared missile.

When we landed I asked the pilot to wait a minute. I called Cassie and said, "Guess what? Tyler and I are in New Mexico." She thought we were still nearby somewhere. "OK if we stay here until Tuesday?" So, with $20 and a credit card in my pocket, we rented a car, stayed at a motel, and visited the famous Carlsbad Caverns on Sunday. On Monday, Tyler joined me in the hanger watching the Air Force set up the plane for the night test. The next day, after getting debriefed in the hanger, we flew commercial back to Los Angeles. Tyler thought I had a pretty neat job at Hughes. Oh yes… the lock-on with the Maverick FLIR and the transfer to a Maverick missile was successful.

Finally the IIR Maverick was set to go into full-scale engineering development. Congressional staff asked the Pentagon to explain why there was no competition for this multimillion-dollar development. Air Staff didn't really know why either, so they asked Wright-Patterson. They, in turn, had me prepare a written explanation of why there was no competition. I guess our sole-source game plan a few years earlier panned out.

The Air Force Maverick program manager in Dayton asked if I would stay on during the full-scale development phase. I said thanks, but no, my contributions were best made in the early formative phases. However, I did take on one more task for them that may have been a first. When the Air Force sent Hughes the request for IIR Maverick, I didn't like the specifications, which looked like those for a TV seeker rather than an infrared seeker. With only my marketing buddy as a confidant, I went back to Dayton and explained it all to the colonel: "Look, our Hughes Maverick program office has taken over the program. Within days they will have tooled up maybe 200 engineers on it. And you will have your equivalent guys also working on IIR Maverick. Your specifications are not quite right, but with all this momentum building up, it will be difficult to fix the requirements, and I will not have the ability to change things." He asked what we should do. I said, "Withdraw the request for the proposal, give me three or four of your best engineers, have them spend a month with our guys, rewrite the specifications, and then resubmit your request for a proposal." In other words, I was suggesting they cancel a major sole-source program with my company. He did just that and followed through as I suggested. I never told the Hughes Maverick program office, let along senior corporate management, what had happened to scuttle the request for our proposal.

Eventually the IIR Maverick went into the Air Force inventory alongside the TV Maverick. In 1990 5,000 TV and IIR Mavericks were launched during Operation Desert Storm, with a success rate of 85 percent. That's over 4,000 targets destroyed. It was a short war.

A COUPLE OF ROUGH SPOTS

There were essentially two types of air-to-ground missile guidance systems. The missiles designed by the Canoga Park engineers used a guidance seeker contained in the missile, such as the missiles I have been describing, and were launched from the attack aircraft. The missiles designed by the Culver City engineers used a guidance system self-contained in the launch aircraft and then directed the missile to the target without a sensor in the missile. This was a natural division of efforts, as Culver City engineers worked on aircraft sensors and Canoga Park did not.

Well, after several years, our guidance-in-the-missile team was winning missile programs, while our counterparts in Culver City were not. The time came to merge the two missile engineering teams. The Culver City team came out and joined us in Canoga Park. That made sense, but man for man, without any exceptions that I can remember, when there were two of us currently holding the same position, the new-to-Canoga-Park guy got the job, and his equivalent Canoga Park pioneer guy like me got the assistant's position. And so I became an assistant to my newly arrived Culver City equivalent.

After several years, the better of the various managers seemed to break through. I felt I was ready to break through, but it wasn't apparent it was going to happen. So, after sufficient frustration with the situation, I went to my boss (a Culver City guy), put my Hughes badge on the table, and said, "Either give me the responsibilities I want, or you can have my badge." Sort of take it or leave it. This caused more excitement than I had expected. When the division manager heard about it, he gave some directions to his intermediates. My boss came back and said, "Scott, you are putting a gun to my head." I retorted, "Your head…it is my job that is on the table, not yours." Since I've didn't retire until 25 years later, I guess I got what I was demanding.

I'll give just one other situation whose origins have to some extent the same roots as the above story. Several years after the above was resolved to my satisfaction, there came a time to consolidate two operations, my laboratory and another fellow's laboratory, thus creating a need for laboratories management. This involved promotions for me and the other fellow. However, I became the "assistant," or perhaps it was "associate," laboratories manager, and he became the laboratories manager, just one step short of becoming an assistant division manager. Yes, he was from the new-to-Canoga Park group. We got along just fine and respected each other's talents, and I learned from him.

Unfortunately, my counterpart had a mild stroke, I believe it was, that took him out for about half a year. I took over the combined operations while he was recuperating. When he came back, he thanked me for not reorganizing operations to my way of doing things, leaving him essentially the ability to easily retain his old job. I remember telling him that I wanted the next promotion but felt it was not fair to compete with him while he was in a hospital, so I was waiting until he got back.

TYLER'S BOMB

In the late 1960s and early 1970s, the war in Vietnam had become increasingly unpopular, particularly with the younger generations and peace-loving people such as my wife. I'm not sure exactly when our son Tyler, tuned into the times, must have been listening to the dinner-table discussions Cassie and I were having regarding my work on air-to-surface missiles, which are bombs. With the clarity of insight of children, Tyler drew a bomb that suited both Cassie and me. Tyler's idea was to build a bomb that would break open upon impact, dispelling seeds that would be planted in the dirt and be watered to make nice flowers. I don't have his original drawing, but it is still clear in my mind, so I'll draw Tyler's bomb from memory.

An illustration of Tyler's bomb is in the color photo section.

A PHONE CALL

Hughes Aircraft was divided into major groups, each made up of divisions. I was in the Aeronautical Systems Group. Among others, there were the Space Systems Group, the Ground Systems Group, and the Industrial Electronics Group (IEG). I didn't really know much about the other groups, and IEG least of all. In September 1975 I got a call from someone in IEG. I didn't know who he was, but as we talked on the phone, I rapidly scanned the Hughes phone book. His organizational code was 9 followed by all zeros. This meant he must be the top dog in the Industrial Electronics Group; IEG was the components group within the company. He wanted me to interview for a job in IEG that day; he said he had permission from corporate. He had gotten my name from a friend at corporate who knew I felt stymied by the politics of Canoga Park.

I was scheduled that afternoon to brief a major general who had come in from Sweden, so I asked the fellow on the phone if we could put it off awhile. He said he really wanted to do it that day. Well, what the heck. I got someone else to brief the general and drove down to Torrance to meet Bill Christoffers of IEG, generally called Chris. I could have written a book about what I didn't know about IEG. We had lunch and spent an interesting afternoon in his office. The job would give me a company car and a salary boost. I would have three research centers reporting to me with lots of Ph.D. engineers and scientists, and the title of Technical Director for IEG.

In response I said, "Well, for starters, I like to tease technical directors just for fun. And your research centers are all dealing in semiconductors. Since quantum electron dynamics solved the physics of electrons, I spent my time in graduate school worrying about nuclear forces and didn't follow the development of semiconductors. And I'm having fun doing what I'm already doing. What else should I say?"

Chris said, "OK, everything I just said would be one-third of your job. You figure out what the rest of the job is. We will share Dolly as our secretary with your office next to mine. You can drop in on any discussion I'm having with my division managers. And, as for semiconductors, I'm sure you will pick it up quickly; it's not that hard." I asked for a day to decide. The next day I accepted the job.

Cassie noted with pleasure that the offer came from someone with the last name CHRISToffers. By the way, Chris was more properly addressed as Dr. Christoffers, in keeping with the academic tradition maintained at Hughes, where I was Dr. Walker. Dr. Christoffers in turn reported to Dr. Allen Puckett at corporate. During most of my career at Hughes, I reported to a hierarchal line of Ph.Ds. The titles were used for the same effect as medical physicians use their titles in their profession.

CHAPTER TWO: 1975–1988

COMPONENT OPERATIONS

TECHNICAL DIRECTOR

GETTING CORPORATE AGREEMENT

One last hurdle keeping me from accepting the offer to transfer to the Industrial Electronics Group turned out to be corporate. My old division manager, Quent McKenna, had given permission for Chris to interview me because he never believed I would take a job in component operations. After learning I had agreed to a transfer to IEG, Quent complained to corporate. As a result, corporate decided to keep me in Canoga Park, and Chris was called in to corporate the next morning and told he couldn't have me. Fortunately, Pat Hyland, the general manager, dropped by Dr. Puckett's office and asked if anyone had talked to me, which they hadn't.

I was called in later that morning, and it was obvious where they were heading, with remarks such as, "You know Hughes is basically a systems house, not a component supplier, and we need you in our principal business," etc. When it was my turn, I said, "Well, first of all, I want this new job." That seemed to work pretty well. And then to push a little further, "I don't know who would replace me in Canoga Park, but I'm sure whoever it is would be glad to see the back of me." (Actually I did; it should be Bob Knowles.) And finally I went for the throat, "Allen (Dr. Puckett), you came to Hughes in the '40s as an aerodynamist and solved the aerodynamics of the Falcon missiles." He said, "That's right. I made the Falcon fly." I finished with, "I don't know how it happens, but today we can hire a young aerodynamicist straight out of college, and he would understand second-order buzz effects for the missile, something you probably never even tried to analyze. Each generation take us farther along; just make room for them. And someone will come along to take my place." It worked.

It was September 1975, and I became technical director for the Industrial Electronics Group. My career working on missiles was over.

RESEARCH CENTERS

I couldn't have taken a job within Hughes that was less like anything I had done so far. I hardly knew what components our system hardware guys needed and certainly didn't much care where they got them. But now, I was in the Industrial Electronics Group, and they dealt with components.

There were three research centers: one in Torrance, one in Newport Beach, and the third further south in Carlsbad, near San Diego. Each center had its own clean room for semiconductors. The centers had been spun out of Hughes Research Laboratory in Malibu, placing them closer to the respective divisions that would someday take their research to market.

The Torrance Research Center was a leader in advanced solid-state microwave components, particularly at 94 GHz. They resided within the Electron Dynamics Division. The Newport Beach Research Center was developing advanced CMOS (complementary metal-oxide-semiconductor) chip structures while residing within the Newport Division, which had its own CMOS lines. The Carlsbad Research Center was into all sorts of one-of-a-kind, exotic semiconductor devices for space, astronomy, and lord knows what all. They resided alongside a division that had been acquired by Hughes with little in common with the center.

IEG had their annual four-day group offsite meeting in Palm Springs just two weeks after I arrived, an affair Cassie and I enjoyed very much. I was asked to give a talk, mostly to give others a chance to know me better. I chose to clarify the roles and missions of the three research centers, declaring they were to do very advanced research leading to new products for their respective divisions. I thought that would be undisputed and was surprised to discover this was not universally accepted by all the division managers and the research directors. Some saw the centers as stand-alone operations that just happened to be located with a division. I worked on this divergence of views over the next several years with some success, if you exclude Carlsbad.

Our Newport Research Center badly needed a new, updated clean room, so shortly after arriving in IEG, I went to Allen Puckett asking for $2 million for a new clean room. He said, "OK, but get the support of the systems groups first." So I started knocking on group executives' doors and did pretty well except for the Space Systems Group. Dr. Bud Wheelon, their group president, took exception. His position was that the Malibu Research Laboratory could provide sufficient quantities for their satellites and didn't need either the Newport Research Center or the Newport Division. Admittedly, the space programs required only small quantities of radiation hard CMOS on sapphire, which the Malibu Laboratory might be able to provide. Well, we had an impasse, so a meeting to resolve the issue of the new clean room took place in Dr. Puckett's office with Dr. Wheelon along with his technical director and me. Bud never really got started, as Allen started the meeting saying, "I don't care if production is measured in the thousands or just a couple of devices. Production is production, and IEG does production." I got my $2 million. Leaving Allen's office, I could sense Bud was recalibrating his views of Walker, this new tech director at IEG. As I'll discuss later, Dr. Wheelon became president of Hughes and gave me a key promotion in my career.

The centers had some exciting new products. The Torrance Center was a world leader in the early days for high-frequency GaAs microwave devices. The Carlsbad Center was providing high-density charge-coupled devices (CCD) to the astronomy community at fantastic prices. During President Reagan's Star Wars era, they were essential for several classified devices. And the Newport Center had the industry's first non-volatile CMOS memory chip, called FATMOS.

IEG had three subsidiaries that essentially operated as the four divisions in IEG. The Microelectronics Limited subsidiaries in Scotland served the European market with technology support from Newport Beach. After we transferred the research center's FATMOS technology to Scotland, they made some improvements to the structure.

As IEG tech director, I was now on the corporate patent committee and was fast learning this segment of our business. I needed the Scotland operation to hold up on their FATMOS patent until a more fundamental patent was filed by the Newport Research Center; otherwise, our combined patent protection would be compromised. With headstrong scientists in both Newport and Scotland, egos got in the way of this time phasing of patents. Ah, the fun of dealing with scientists.

I sat in on all the monthly division financial reporting sessions. That was better than a year's business school education. Chris, along with his one assistant group executive, Jim Sutherland, and his CFO, John Roberts, were able to manage the $500 million group. They did not slow things down with a large group office staff.

Jim Sutherland had joined the company several years earlier when

Hughes bought his company, which then evolved to become the Carlsbad Division. He had a lovable but cantankerous personality. He could really scare someone who had not handled something properly. I figured Jim out: "You are a hip shooter. Without knowing all the facts, you shoot at the presenter. If you are wrong, they come back at you, and you just move on. If you make a direct hit, you have done some good." He admitted I had it about right. And by shooting a lot he frequently scored direct hits. In 1977 Jim took me to Scotland to visit our Scottish subsidiary, my first trip to Europe. We became good friends, and I learned a lot from him while trying to ignore several of his habits. One tip he gave me was to always try to make some improvement every day, big or small, just improve something every day. I've taken that philosophy with me ever since.

OK, how about the other two-thirds of my time? Chris had said I could define myself when he offered me the job in IEG. He held true to his promise. Here are two examples.

ENERGY CONSERVATION AND GENERATION

Remember the gas shortage in 1973 when the Saudis decided to punish the U.S. for our support of Israel? The U.S. government, perhaps for the first time, was showing itself serious about doing something about our dependency on foreign oil. Among other things the government formed ERDA (Energy Research and Development Administration). I located ways we could help and tried to obtain ERDA funding. The technology pool I considered was not just within IEG but across the entire company.

I located several dozen initiatives. Using cryo-stick technology designed to extract heat from inside satellites, we proposed to pipe heat off automobile engines into the passenger cabin for very rapid warming when the engine is first turned on. The company had already invested in an earth thermo-heat extraction program in northern California for electric generation. Malibu worked on the laser implosion technology for nuclear implosion fusion at Livermore. A subsidiary that provided solar cells for satellites invested for a while in terrestrial solar panels. We had a handheld infrared detector used by firefighters to find people in a fire; this could be used to spot heat losses in buildings. In total, I found maybe another dozen energy conservation or generation programs at

Hughes, with several of the key programs in IEG.

I won't go into detail about the numerous activities I got involved with, but will summarize by saying: ERDA did not turn out to be a source of funding for Hughes. Terrestrial solar cells had application only in locations that otherwise could not be powered (such as ocean buoys), and when the Middle East turned on the oil spigot, most of the attention dissipated. I did not make a significant contribution to our businesses related to the energy shortage. However, I did get a good education on the energy crisis.

MEDICAL ELECTRONICS

The Howard Hughes Medical Institute was set up by Howard Hughes when he spun Hughes Aircraft Company out of Hughes Tool in 1953. [See Apendix A.] The institute wholly owned Hughes Aircraft Company, with the profits going to the institute, which in turn funded medical research, naming medical researchers as Howard Hughes Fellows. To insure the arrangement was not some sort of tax avoidance scheme for medical products to be exploited by Hughes Aircraft Company based on institute-funded research, we were directed to stay out of the field. In fact, Howard Hughes had specifically stated that Hughes Aircraft was not to be in the medical field.

Nevertheless, I noted two things had changed by the late '70s. After protracted litigation, the IRS had to concede that the relationship between the aircraft company and the institute was legitimate and taxes were being paid properly. And Hughes, the sole trustee of the institute, had died. I reasoned we should now be able to enter the medical electronics industry with Hughes Aircraft technologies, just not make use of the rather esoteric research of the Hughes Fellows.

So, I went to corporate with this observation and got $500,000 to proceed. The president understood I needed some "walking around money" if I were to entice our engineers to go after electronic medical devices. I joined the biomedical instruments association and started to learn the trade.

About this time, I felt I needed an assistant and successfully argued for an assistant technology director. Don Calhoun, a talented Ph.D. from one of the systems divisions, joined me in the group office. I'm not sure, but it is possible this was the first time any group had an assistant tech director.

I felt like the Pied Piper. Everywhere I went there were engineers anxious to have an opportunity to work on medical products. To name several projects: we proposed to use digital pattern recognition to rapidly reduce Holter monitor readouts, which in those days still required a tech to scan through a day's worth of EKG tapes. Another proposal was for a semiconductor device that could provide certain readings of blood samples. Still another was a high-frequency ultrasonic microscope, in the 100 kilocycle region, for reading biological slides.

My favorite investigator was a Ph.D. Chinese research chemist at the Malibu Research Lab. He had just become a medical doctor as well. What a find. He wanted to invent ways to offer better medical support to people who had limited resources. One of his ideas was a visual stethoscope for the general practitioner. The cardiologist in his well-equipped laboratory can look at monitor scope of a patient's heartbeat. The general practitioner, however, only hears the heartbeat through his stethoscope. But as he or she gets older, the doctor may no longer hear critical faint sounds. The visual stethoscope added sound processing and a small LCD display to a normal stethoscope. The doctor could view the sound wave pattern in addition to listening to the sound. Keep in mind that in the '70s, all of this was pushing the technology, and our Newport Beach division had all the key technologies: CMOS, hybrid circuits, and liquid crystal displays.

We built a prototype of the visual stethoscope that fitted in a briefcase. After sufficient testing, we planned to reduce the electronics to a chip. I flew back east to offer a major manufacturer of stethoscopes an exclusive license if we were successful in the development. I learned something rather interesting. These stethoscope manufacturers said cardiologists would not want GPs to have this capability. Since cardiology was a large market for them, they didn't want to get involved with our project. We needed to find another outlet.

However, our effort to develop and license medical instruments was interrupted by an event: I was promoted to manager of the Newport Beach division. The gentleman who took over as the group's technical director was not in favor of pursing the medical market, and the medical device program was terminated.

There is a satisfying story, however, related to the chemist/MD and the visual stethoscope. While working emergency calls in China-town, he was called to a street accident and brought our suitcase proto-type with him. Using the device, he detected the person had a serious heart problem. Furthermore, the fellow had passed his annual physical just a few days earlier. I was told, after my associate had identified the problem using the visual stethoscope, the guy went through a heart operation that saved his life.

SOLID STATE PRODUCTS DIVISION

The division at Newport Beach was split into two parts, with the new division moving to a location near the Orange County airport, maybe eight miles away. Newport would continue with components: semiconductors, hybrid microcircuits, and an aging product line for quartz crystal oscillators and filters.

The new division was named Microelectronics Division and would manage the small systems that incorporated Newport's components. Along with other products, they were leaders in multiplex audio sys-tems for commercial airlines and had a program for centralized display controls and a security system for the new Smithsonian Air Museum in Washington, DC. Most of the assembly was done in Mexicali, Mexico, where in addition to their own products the division manufactured an advanced frequency-hopping military radio for the Hughes Ground Systems Group.

Chris gave me the choice of the division I wanted: components or the new Microelectronics Division. If I had just joined IEG after working on large military systems for fourteen years, I would have undoubtedly chosen the Microelectronics Division. But now I better understood what the core mission of our group was: supplying key components to the large systems groups. For that reason, I chose New-port Beach, renaming the division the Solid State Products Division. Bill Mueller, who had been the Newport division manager, transferred to the new Microelectronics Division.

Thank goodness for the education in business management I had garnered from sitting in on the division monthly reporting sessions for three years; otherwise I would have bombed out. Until this point, I had always been involved in developing new products for the future, not making a here-and-now profit. A profit and loss (P&L) division such as I was now taking on also had to develop new products while making a profit each year. There were a lot of differences.

The two assistant division managers in the Solid State Products Division were Karl Reismueller for hybrid microcircuits and Dick Belardi for semiconductors. Both senior managers had the technical base and experience that was invaluable to the division. We developed a close friendship that continues to this day.

The move to Newport Beach forced a housing relocation. Cassie and I with our three sons, Tyler, Morgan, and Brandon, moved from our historic Homewood in La Cañada Flintridge to Newport Beach. We found a nice, newly constructed house on Balboa Peninsula, ten minutes from work. All three sons had loved our beautiful Homewood and said no way were they going to leave; however, moving to a location only a few feet from the bay and a hundred yards from the ocean soon changed their minds. Perhaps what I liked most is that for the rest of their time in school, I was always available during the work day.

The mission for the Solid State Products Division was not simple. Our main reason for existence was to supply critical components for Hughes systems. Outside business was a means to an end. It was OK to sell on the outside; in fact, it was absolutely necessary in order to have the volume needed to mature products and to be competitive. The quantities needed for Hughes systems, particularly for semiconductors, was just not large enough. This is a classical conundrum for many internal component suppliers.

I was the tenth manager of the Newport Beach division since it had been formed twenty years earlier. I asked my secretary for photos of each of the past nine managers, as I only knew personally the last manager. For fun, she added a tenth photo to the set, a photo of me. I laid all ten photos out on my conference table and studied them, wanting to better understand their personalities. What did they do right? What did they do wrong? Though each of them had some marks of success, the truth was that the division was now not well regarded. It was in fairly poor condition physically, organizationally, and technically. We had union problems; the middle management was top heavy. Semiconductors were losing their importance to Hughes systems. And, at least in my opinion, none of the previous managers had really been successful in leveraging their careers upward within Hughes after leaving

Newport Beach. Where had they gone wrong? Lots of reasons, but for me, the most fundamental was not finding the proper balance between supplying components to Hughes and chasing external business.

DIGITAL WATCHES

If you didn't already know, I suspect you would be surprised to learn that by the mid-'70s, the Newport Beach division made one-third of all U.S. digital watch modules. The modules were sold to Timex, Sears, Bulova, and about seven other U.S. watch companies. The first company in Switzerland to manufacture digital watches, located in Neuchâtel, got started with a digital watch license from Newport Beach. They became the original supplier internal to Switzerland for the SWATCH watch.

Certainly the most successful of the external endeavors of Newport Beach during the early and mid-'70s was digital watch modules. But as for all consumer products, supply usually catches up to demand, and prices for any product start to drop. The group deserves credit for being aggressive and driving cost down to meet the competition. In fact, a major reason the Microelectronics Division was formed was to better focus on digital watches. Sometimes only half in jest, I would refer to the new division as the "Watch Division." Assembly was moved to their maquiladora (across the border) facility in Mexicali and out of Newport Beach. This starved off the profit losses for awhile. Then assembly was moved to Taipei to further reduce cost.

We tried to engineer advanced versions as a way to demand better margins. In particular I remember as tech director sitting at the back of the room during one of those monthly finance meetings when the watch team said they were going to produce a digital calculator watch. The module price would be such that Sears could sell it for $100 or could discount it to $60 as a store special. Now, in those days a typical chip layout might take up to a year, but this time they did an exceptionally fast design and got the calculator watch into production in only six months.

I was again sitting at the back of the room as tech director when the watch product line manager had to inform the group that to meet competition, they would have to introduce the digital calculator watch to the market at a loss. In my log book, I wrote, "The digital watch is dead. It's all over." We could not advance design ourselves back into profit.

I also had my hand in trying to design an advanced digital watch. While I was tech director working on medical electronics, we built a digital pulse watch. The wearer places a finger on two dimples on the lower part of the watch. One dimple has an infrared pulse source. The other dimple reads the return pulse coming from the finger. When fresh, oxygenated blood goes through the finger, the infrared is more absorbed, hence the momentary dip in the readout. I think that is also how a finger-clip pulse reader works, as at the hospital when the nurse wants to keep track of your pulse over a period of time. We built two "pulse watches." The project never went forward, but today I still have a "$250,000 pulse watch" in my drawer.

Texas Instruments was the prime cost cutter in the market. As was typical for TI, they would "forward price," selling at first for a loss but gaining major market share. Then, using volume, they would drive the cost down below this price within a year, own the market, and start making good profits. But this time it didn't work; TI lost a bundle of money. So did National Semiconductor and all the others. After the bubble burst, all production was essentially offshore. By the time it all ended, our losses matched what we had earned. Other companies would have been glad to break even as we did.

Taking over the Solid State Products Division, I now faced the problem that watch chip volume went down as the new Microelectronics Division started shutting down watch operations. Our CMOS semiconductor line, which had expanded to meet the volume demands of our digital watch modules, was now losing money. The situation was aggravated by the fact that the semiconductor product line had lost its focus of being of value to Hughes systems as they pursued the digital watch market.

A little side story on closing down the watch operations: on the way home from Japan, Chris suggested I drop by a small company in Taipei that still owed us $75,000 for capital equipment he had placed there during the time they assembled our digital watches. Knowing the company would be on hard times, Chris said, "Don't be too hard on them, but pick up the money." The owner had died, and his charming daughter now ran the place. She drove me to her plant out in the Chinese countryside, where about 200 girls worked on the assembly line and were housed in a dormitory, a typical arrangement. You could see how watch module prices had fallen. Bless her, she was selling modules to a middle man in Hong Kong for $1.25 a watch; we would have gotten $20 only a few years earlier.

The evening after visiting the facility, she graciously hosted a nice dinner where there were toasts around the table. In China you don't toast everybody all at once; you select someone to toast and while looking into their eyes, take a sip. Later that person would likely toast you back. Looking into the lovely young owner's brown eyes and toasting her, I would sort of melt.

The next morning, as my airplane was accelerating down the runway, it came to me: I had totally forgotten to ask for the 75K. The following day, my CFO in Newport asked if I had gotten the money, as it was still on the books. I said, "Shut up and write it off."

BIPOLAR DEVICES

Slacking sales for CMOS wasn't all of our semiconductor woes. We also had a bipolar semiconductor line that was hopelessly outdated with inadequate facilities and inadequate management. Bipolar semiconductors are a type of semiconductor device different from CMOS; they are semiconductors that are capable of handling high voltages and are very fast acting, making bipolar devices particularly useful in radars and high performance computers. As CMOS devices improved in speed and used less power, bipolar semiconductors applications eventually became less important. Yet, at the same time, the Newport Beach division, with the help of the Radar Division in one of the systems groups, was working hard on an advanced bipolar semiconductor structure that was leading edge. If ever the Newport Beach division was out of sync with a Hughes systems requirement, this was it. With help from the Radar Division, our bipolar department had gotten Amdahl Corporation interested in using our advanced bipolar devices in their next generation of large computers. Amdahl, a fairly new computer company, was taking on IBM head to head, not with small computers but with top-of-the-line ones, and they were having some success. In fact, Hughes information systems were already buying from Amdahl instead of IBM for our mainframe computers.

By the time I arrived, Amdahl Corporation had contracted with Newport Beach for our advanced bipolar devices for their next-generation computers. I visited Gene Amdahl in the Bay Area to understand what was going on. The truth was that without a massive new influx of funding and much more time than was presently available, we would never be able to serve Amdahl or Hughes Radar Division. Trouble was brewing.

Before long, Amdahl sent his head of purchasing and a lawyer down to Newport to talk with me. I was somewhat apprehensive that they might be thinking of suing us for causing them to miss their next-generation mainframe computer. Instead, they simply wanted to terminate the contractual arrangement for convenience, not cause. I said OK, but asked them to let us continue until the end of the following week to finish the last semiconductor batch. We would submit our final bill and give them whatever came out of the last run. They were happy; I was very happy. Not long afterwards, I shut down the entire bipolar product line. The operation was just too far gone to try to recover it.

TOY MARKET

While we were drawing down the watch chip business, my external CMOS market manager said we should go after the newly emerging chip market for toys. I said, "Toys. Are you're crazy?" He told me, "The toy market will be different than the digital watch market because watches became a hot commodity with a number of suppliers supplying the same things: four, five, or six function chips. Instead, the toy firms, new to the chip game, will design us into their product and, at least in the beginning, won't be able to drag prices down with competition. As a plus, New England toy companies (perhaps unlike Mattel in California) behave more like dignified, old-world companies." Since we really needed replacement business, I went along.

Milton Bradley was our principal target. We supplied millions of chips for such toys as Simon, Battleship, and various hand-held games. The only time we got in trouble was when the price of gold skyrocketed, going from a few hundred to eight hundred dollars an ounce. We bonded the chips using gold wire and were caught dead footed because we hadn't yet learned to account for the rapidly increasing cost of gold. So I called the CEO of Milton Bradley, with whom I had become friends, and explained that for this year's Christmas market we would lose $500,000 because of the unexpected rise in the price of gold. He asked if we would be making additional profit if we revised our several contracts for the rise in the price of gold. I said no. He said, "OK, I'll give you the 500." Our marketing manager was right; there were some fine gentlemen in the New England toy industry.

The lucrative consumer toy-chip business finally ended for us when National came out with an inexpensive four-bit microprocessor. That changed the game. Now a toy was defined by software, not a custom chip. We got into the toy market, made some money, and got out whole.

SEMICONDUCTOR GATE ARRAYS

Dick Belardi, the assistant division manager for semiconductors, took on the challenging task of repositioning the product to better serve the internal Hughes market. This required two things: faster speeds and faster design turnaround times. With fresh capital funding from the company, Dick was able to reduce line widths from 3.0 microns to 1.2 microns, which for the time yielded respectable speed.

Equally important, we got into gate arrays, which really changed the whole ball game. With gate arrays, a standard chip is designed with as many unconnected gate arrays as can fit on it. We had a 20,000-gate chip, which for a while was considered large. Then, using our custom computer software, you could connect the arrays to make a logic chip. We were one of the early leaders in this field, causing IBM to run an advertisement featuring the Solid State Products Division using their computers for gate-array design. Before long, though, we changed over to DEC computers.

At last, we could quickly design and ship high-performance custom CMOS circuits in small quantities at a reasonable cost, exactly what Hughes and the external market wanted. We set up a fancy modern design lab in Newport Beach where we taught Hughes systems engineers how to use our software, enabling them do the designs themselves. I started to believe we had at last reached the promising land of a CMOS semiconductor capability matched to the company needs.

I guess I should have known better. Gate arrays and modern computer design software changed the game for the external semiconductor suppliers, as well. In particular, a business leader named Wilf Corrigan also recognized the dynamic changes in the custom circuit market, forming LSI Logic Corporation in the Bay Area, and proceeded to market Hughes heavily. They were willing to meet the same small-quantity needs of Hughes systems, something the external suppliers in the past were reluctant to do. I visited with Wilf several times looking for a way to form some sort of friendly relationship. The effort was without success, as I needed corporate backing and didn't get it. So we had a competitive market on our hands again. Shucks. Semiconductors are a very aggressive market that never lets up. Before long, the 20,000 gates gave way to 100,000 gates and channel widths of 0.9 microns and would not stop there, all requiring new rounds of investment.

OFFSHORE ASSEMBLY

We moved commercial chip packaging to the Philippines and stationed an expatriate (an American citizen living in another country) there along with his wife to coordinate with our subcontractor. The subcontracting relationship proved to be quite satisfactory. I made several trips, usually on the way back from Japan, and always enjoyed my stays, which included visiting Cassie's niece and her husband, Mike Ballast, and their children.

Jerome, Cassie's oldest brother, had been a missionary to the Philippines for many years. His daughter married a missionary, and at that time they lived in metro Manila. One night Mike took me to a poverty-stricken area and showed me the conditions under which he and his wife were trying to help the locals, both body and soul. I would have never dared to go into that area alone, but with him we were welcomed and safe.

The owner of the subcontracting company invited Karl Reismueller, my assistant division manager; Andre Kobel, our new international marketing manager; and me to go sailing on a Saturday. I hesitated because I wanted to be home for Brandon's piano recital; still, I said OK. He had his captain and crew sail all night, leaving the Manila harbor so as to position his 78-foot ketch, the *Blackjack*, at a small harbor on the west coast of Luzon. Going on board I noticed he was carrying a large, heavy suitcase. Andre informed me that it contained the ammunition for the arsenal he maintained on board. This was illegal under President Ferdinand Marcos, but still not a bad idea in pirate-infested seas.

We headed out to a small island in the South China Sea to anchor, snorkel, and have lunch onboard. On the way out to the island, I noticed the captain using his binoculars to watch a junk about a mile away that was on a course across our path. Without saying anything, he steered our boat off to the right and watched to see if the junk also changed course. It didn't. If it had changed course to again cross our path, I'm sure the captain would have turned on the motors, opened the suitcase, and headed for home. The threat of piracy passed.

The crew had some fun with Karl and me by strapping us into a bosun's (boatswain's) chair. Then they heeled the boat over on a broad reach, and left us dangling high up out over the water. They particularly enjoyed dunking me several times and then pulling me back up.

Figuring I could take a red-eye home from the Philippines and just maybe make it to Brandon's performance, I hopped aboard a plane and got to the recital, already underway, just as Brandon came out to play. Fortunately, as the best of the performers, he was playing last. When the performances were over, there was a reception at the host's beautiful home on the mesa overlooking the Newport harbor. Someone asked where I had been. I said as casually as I could, "Oh, I've been sailing in the South China Sea."

Wilf Corrigan at LSI Logic was the first to bring to my attention that the Philippines were a disaster waiting to happen because President Marcos was fast losing public support. Wilf was pulling out. I decided to follow suit and chose Singapore, more expensive but clearly more stable. Our expat liked the Philippines and hated Singapore, but he went anyway. In fact, he was in Singapore setting things up when the revolution happened with his wife still in Manila. On the Saturday of the revolution, she took a dive to the floor of their apartment as military jets flew over. Turned out it was a victory flyby, not a strafing pass. It took two or three days before we were able to make phone contact with her.

Marcos went into exile in Hawaii. The problem now was that the Philippine communists tried to disrupt business with the capitalistic world, especially the U.S., using violence to make it happen. I was glad we moved operations to Singapore, but eventually things settled down again in Manila, though not in the southern islands.

Singapore is something else. Orchard Road, the main drag, has as fancy a collection of stores as Rodeo Drive in Beverly Hills. At the time Delco Electronics, which was now part of Hughes Electronics, had 2,400 employees in Singapore assembling automobile radios. I dropped by their plant to let the manager know I was setting up chip packaging subcontracting there. The town is very safe, beautiful, and industrious. Just don't try to find any foreign newspapers critical of the government.

EUROPEAN MARKET
The external semiconductor sales manager who got us into the toy market left and was replaced with a new Swiss-born guy. Andre convinced me we should be selling direct in Europe, so we opened an office in Munich. This was all a new experience for me.

However, Industrial Electronics Group (IEG) already had a subsidiary located in Scotland. Microelectronics Limited reported to the IEG group office just like the divisions. They rightly saw themselves as Hughes Aircraft in Europe for, among other things, semiconductors, and here was Newport showing up in Europe also selling semiconductors. This was very disconcerting to Ian Duffin, the managing director. Ian and I were pretty good friends, and perhaps out of kindness to me, he directed his anger more towards Dick Belardi, the assistant division manager and product line manager for semiconductors. I tried to resolve the conundrum in the most gentlemanly of manners. At a European marketing meeting we were having in Paris, I took Ian and Dick to the Crazy Horse to talk it all over. Somehow the issue didn't get resolved there.

A year later, with the conflict still not resolved, we were having a U.S. marketing meeting in New Orleans. Out on the street in the French Quarter one evening, Ian, Dick, and I again had an intense discussion about who should be marketing in Europe. A streetwalker came by trying to generate some business of her own type, but just shook her head and walked away as it was clear the three of us were far more interested in our own business objectives. I noted that the bar had made us put our drinks in paper cups to go out on the street. It appeared that the only thing illegal in the French Quarter was glass cups on the street.

Well, another year rolled by, and Ian came to California to resolve the marketing-in-Europe problem once and for all. He did not want Newport Beach in Europe selling semiconductors, period. We had a quiet dinner on Balboa Island still trying to find some common ground, to no avail. The next day we met with Chris, president of the Industrial Electronics Group and our common boss. Chris listened and then said, "All right, Ian, you can have the European market exclusively. And, Ian, you now report to Scott instead of me." He had taken care of the problem in a way that was a surprise, especially to me.

HUGHES MICROELECTRONICS LIMITED

To better coordinate the two operations, we formed Microelectronics Operations, composed of Ian's Hughes Microelectronics Limited (HML) in Scotland and the Solid State Products Division in Newport Beach that I had been heading. I had visited HML a number of times over the last ten years and developed a real liking for the people.

One year Cassie, the three boys, and I vacationed in Great Britain over the Christmas holidays. We celebrated Hogmanay (New Year) in the small Scottish town of Auchtermuchty, home of Sandy Marshal, a key executive at HML. That particular year, one second was to be added to keep the earth's orbit in sync with the atomic clocks. Just before midnight, I went up the tower at the town square with the mayor to ring in the New Year and convinced him to take a deep breath and wait for one second before ringing the bell. He probably thought I was nuts, which may have been about right.

Everyone broke out a little flask to celebrate their neighbors, and then we moved on to yet another of the houses, which invited us in. Son Morgan, a good-looking college kid from California, took a liking to the cute Scottish girls, who returned the favor. So rather than go with us to the next house, he said he would stay on at the town square. Well, around 2 AM we remembered Morgan and had our driver take us back to the square. There sitting on the curb in a deserted square was a rather lonesome Morgan, glad to see us.

Another fond memory from the days when I had the responsibility of overseeing our Scottish subsidiary is a meeting held at a charming old lodge on the Isle of Arran off the coast of Scotland near Glasgow. John Roberts, the CFO of IEG, and I, were present, and our wives were in attendance, as were a number of key HML managers and their wives. The meeting was both productive and of very positive value in bonding these distant cousins with their southern California relatives. Bagpipes, haggis and neaps, and single-malt scotch were the order of the day.

HML won an important military contract with the U.K. government, which resulted in my joining Ian to welcome Michael Heseltine, the Secretary of State for Defense, to our plant in Glenrothes, Scotland. Over lunch I engaged him in a discussion about USSR President Mikhail Gorbachev's efforts at perestroika (reform). I argued Gorbachev was only trying to modernize the Communist government; Heseltine, who had been with Gorbachev the past week, contended Gorbachev was no longer a Communist but simply had to frame things the way he did. Looking back over history, I still believe I was right. Eventually, Heseltine had a falling out with Margaret Thatcher and was forced to leave her cabinet.

HYBRID MICROCIRCUITS

The Reagan-era military buildup was a major factor in the growing success at Newport Beach as well for the entire company. As a result the hybrid microcircuits product line managed by Karl Reismueller was booming. In fact we got to the point where we had to stop taking new external business because our capacity was filled just handling internal Hughes needs.

In addition to military programs, the hybrid product line was also qualified to build hybrid microcircuits for space programs, which have very strict design and process controls. Before I came to Newport, Karl had transferred hybrid circuit technology under license to a company in Japan jointly owned by Hughes and NEC (Nippon Electric Company). And now, also under license, Karl helped qualify the company to build hybrid circuits for space applications. This Hughes NEC company was the first hybrid microcircuit supplier qualified for space programs in Japan.

The Newport facility was filling to capacity due to the growing hybrid volume as well the additional space needed for new ion implanters, advanced optical lithography, computer expansions, and so forth of the revitalized semiconductor operations. We needed to build a 100,000-square-foot hybrid microcircuits building plus a five-story parking structure. Since this required formal corporate approval, I was back at corporate with hat in hand. The facilities executive who brought me into the capital meeting said to keep it simple and I'd get my money. What they really wanted to discuss that day was a new Gulfstream executive jet. During the discussion of my request, Pat Hyland said, "Scott, raise your right hand and promise if you ever buy land for Hughes, you'll never buy less than 50 acres." Hughes Aircraft had been land poor ever since the early 1950s, when the company was spun out of Hughes Tool without owning the land under the business. Pat wanted to set me going in the right direction.

The $15 million expansion was completed, with the ribbon cutting a year later in February 1984. The expansion gave us four buildings in total. The facility also got a facelift, a new cafeteria, a new executive conference room, new signage out on the street, a new main lobby, updated landscaping, and so forth.

I should give recognition to my wife Cassie for her contributions to the esthetics of the facility in Newport Beach as we made improvements. On more than one occasion, she would tour the facility on a Sunday and offer suggestions. In fact, throughout my career and in so many ways, Cassie always supported me in my work.

The high-voltage power lines on Superior Avenue were on poles. I had always felt that was not in keeping with our image as a modern electronics company, particularly in an upscale location like Newport Beach, so I took the lead to get the power lines put underground. Southern California Edison and the city joined with us and formed a special district starting at the city line on down to Hoag Hospital. It cost Hughes $90,000. I never asked permission, just did it.

To handle the increased parking, we built a five-level parking structure on our 18-acre site. The city was in a "no growth" mood, so it took a lot of talking with the mayor, the city planners, and council members. Apparently, at least to one city planner, if the elevator for the parking structure, which was set back 100 yards from the street, was ten feet higher we would somehow destroy the intrinsic beauty of this commercial manufacturing sector of the city. So to this day, you have to get off on the fourth floor and walk up to the fifth. They also held us up for $250,000 to improve a traffic intersection half mile away due to the increased traffic they envisioned. Their paper study included added traffic out to the Balboa peninsula, which seemed to ignore the fact that I was the only person out on the peninsula that worked at Hughes.

I arranged for an aerial photograph of our newly upgraded facility. My favorite was not the low-altitude shot I had requested, but a high-altitude shot the photographer added. It is in the color photo section of this book.

CIRCUITOS DE BAJA CALIFORNIA FUNDADORES

In addition to expanding operations in Newport Beach, Karl added a maquiladora in Tijuana for hybrid microelectronics. Two other divisions within Industrial Electronics Group already had maquilador operations in Tijuana and Mexicali. A typical maquiladora operates in Mexico near the U.S. border. Material is shipped to the plant for assembly at lower labor rates. The products are then returned to the States for retailing.

A new border crossing had recently opened up about ten miles west of downtown Tijuana, and most of the new maquiladora facilities were being built there. However, the worker turnover was very high, around 20 percent per month, which would not be acceptable for the skilled operators we would need. It appeared to me that although the new border crossing was very convenient for us gringos to visit and go home the same day, the facilities were too far away from where the workers lived.

Instead, we decided to build a plant where the workers lived. We found a beautiful location on top of the hill on Los Fundadores Boulevard in Tijuana. Our assistant facility manager lived there during construction to insure building specifications were met. The building was open for operations in August 1985. Karl asked Ron Shaver, a manager who understood both hybrid circuits and maquiladora operations, to manage the plant. Ron in turn had a capable Mexican engineer to oversee the assembly line along with one or two other Mexican engineers. The total experience was quite satisfactory.

BAUER PATENT

Hughes was in violation of the "001" silicon crystal orientation patent used to make blank wafers for semiconductors, a Fujitsu patent. Essentially everyone was in violation, because we were all using 001 wafers, but since we could not be sued for making devices for the U.S. military programs, only our commercial sales were vulnerable. Fujitsu offered us a paid-up license for $100,000, which probably was reasonable. In the normal course of things in matters of this kind, Hughes sent Fujitsu copies of our numerous semiconductor patents, offering to swap patents instead of cash. This all took place before my time, and I knew nothing about it.

A corporate patent lawyer came down to Newport Beach to get my signature, the last signature needed on a patent swap proposed by Fujitsu. They would settle for $10,000 and one of our patents called the Bauer patent, named after the Hughes scientist who invented it. Our patent attorney was rather excited at saving Hughes $90,000.

Now I'm slow, so I asked what the Bauer patent was. He said it was just one of our old patents from about fourteen years ago with only three years left on it. "OK, but just what is the Bauer patent?" I brought in Dr. Tom Toombs, head of our Newport Research Center, who explained in more detail that it was a process patent on how to manufacture short-channel devices. The patent had been sort of ahead of its time and not particularly useful except for very short device channel widths.

Upon reflection, Tom started to wonder, well, how else would you do short channels? After consultation with his team, he came to the startling realization that, starting with one million-bit memories, the whole world might be in violation of the Bauer patent! Tom deserves a lot of credit for reaching this realization.

A problem with process patents as opposed to product patents is that you can usually just look at a product to tell it violates a product patent. With a process patent, it is much harder, sort of like eating someone's great pastry—not what is it, but how did they bake it? Tom and his team studied Intel and other component suppliers' products trying to figure out how they processed short channels. Not an easy task. Meanwhile, a now-enlightened Hughes patent office sent a notice to all the major semiconductor companies announcing that we believed they might be in violation of the enclosed Bauer patent and should consider taking a license. This started the clock. Since there were only a few years left on the patent, the timing of these notices was all important.

Finally, we came to the inescapable conclusion that indeed Intel and others were using the Bauer process. We contacted Motorola with an offer for a paid-up license. They said no thanks. That was an error; the price went up for them later. We then contacted IBM. To their credit it took only about a week for them to agree, but IBM added, by the way, a list of thousands of patents that we might be in violation of. They paid us $5 million, we paid them $3.5 million, and we swapped patent portfolios.

That set the net for the big fish. For us to be injured by the violation of one of our patents, we needed to lose revenue because of the violation. We weren't selling enough commercially to be all that injured. But for IBM, our patent licensee, that was an entirely different matter. Since IBM had a large commercial market, then another supplier in violation of the Bauer patent harmed the market value for our licensee.

Japan had become the world's largest supplier of memory chips. Unfortunately we did not have patent coverage in Japan for the Bauer process. But they certainly were injuring IBM's business with their imports to the United States. After delays and more delays, it became clear the Japanese companies would not get serious until a senior Hughes executive was directly involved. So Chris went to Japan and on a Monday told them to sign up or on Friday, before he departed, Hughes would request the U.S. government to embargo their imports that were in violation of the Bauer patent. Chris flew home Friday with the Japanese suppliers agreeing to pay out $13 million.

Yet Intel was the main target. The rest of the U.S. industry kind of hid behind Intel, waiting to see if we would get Intel to sign up. Things dragged out, well beyond the last three years of the patent, but no matter, the clock was ticking for all of them because they had all been put on notice. Well, Hughes won a court judgment over Intel and got $30 million. The rest then folded and paid up. When it was all added up, the Bauer patent brought in $78,554,348 for Hughes from 28 companies.

My main contribution was declining to sign the original proposal from Fujitsu, having our research team determine the value of the Bauer patent, and getting the ball rolling. And thank you Fujitsu for reading our patents, because we didn't know what we had.

UNION ISSUES

As a trombone player and manager of a thirteen-piece dance band while I was in college, I was a member of the American Federation of Musicians. This was my only direct experience with labor unions until I came to Newport Beach. When addressing union members, I often started by noting my union membership. Nevertheless, I had union problems, complicated by poor advice I received from my human resources manager.

Division management had allowed poor labor union relations to develop over a period of time. Not long after I arrived, the union decided to file as many grievances, real or trivial, that it could find. The idea apparently was to force arbitration, which usually gave the union some net gains. The advice I was given was to just ignore the grievances, as they would be eventually thrown out. And worse, the advice I was getting was to not get involved directly by talking to the union president, whom I had never met.

After this went on for several years, I'd had it with this advice. I called the union president and asked to have dinner with him. Over a nice meal, he said, "With your all-time high number of grievances against your operation, you must be ready to be fired about now." I said, "Are you kidding? I just made group vice president today." I added that if he was as interested in the well-being of our employees as I was, we would get along just fine.

We held a successful cocktail party for the local union leaders and my senior staff. Not long afterwards, two leaders of the local union branch asked for the afternoon off to attend a lecture on union issues up in Los Angeles. I said OK, if they let me go with them. After the lecture, we had dinner in Chinatown. Arriving back to the plant late that evening, I lent one of them my company car to go home, as he had missed his car pool. The next morning he enjoyed tossing my car keys on the receptionist's desk as much as I did hearing about it.

Each year we held a lunch at the Balboa Bay Club for employees who had submitted cost improvement suggestions. That particular year, I asked the union president to be my guest speaker. He told the employees, "Your job is to make money for the company. My job is to get that money into your pockets." I commented that that was just about right. We became friends, and most of the four hundred grievances were cancelled, while we did agree to a few without ever getting an arbitrator involved.

SCHOLARSHIPS

The Hughes Management Club sponsored scholarships for the children of Hughes employees. The scholarships were based on scholastic achievement, not need. (After all, the kids' parents worked at Hughes.) While working in Canoga Park, I was asked to manage the program. Essays from the candidates were submitted to our committee, which in turn reduced the list to six students. We then invited a couple of professors from the University of Southern California to interview the finalists and to pick two awardees. We were prepared to take their recommendations, period. Reading the essays and seeing these brilliant senior high school students on the Saturday of the interviews was quite an enjoyable experience.

Having had some experience with the management club scholarship program, I decided to champion something similar for the School of Engineering at UC Irvine (UCI). The School of Engineering was filling its quota with good students, but the top two percent were going to Stanford, Berkeley, and UCLA, not UCI. I noted that all the scholarships available for the School of Engineering were based on need, none on merit alone.

I got the UCI Engineering School Business Support Group, which I was heading at the time, to fund four-year scholarships for two of the best students applying to the UCI School of Engineering, awards based solely on merit. These students almost assuredly would have offers from the other top schools as well. We named the scholarship after the founding head of the School of Engineering at UCI, Robert M. Saunders. This time, we let UCI sort through the candidates and make the selections.

In addition to the Engineering School Business Support Group, I became a member of the university's Founders Club, and the Chancellor's Business Alliance organization. The latter was an idea of Chancellor Jack Peltason, who later became president of the University of California system. The Chancellor's Business Alliance had great offsite meetings each year, giving us opportunities to get to know various professors, meet other business executives in Orange County, and offer advice to the chancellor. The offsites were always a lot of fun. One affair in the Monterey area was a '60s night at which we were to dress in the style of hippies. I think Cassie and I might have won first prize that evening.

I was asked to give the keynote address at the groundbreaking for a new building for the School of Engineering at UCI. In the appendix, I've included my talk, which elicited an unusually favorable response due mostly to my last topic in the presentation.

ACQUISITION BY GENERAL MOTORS

Howard Hughes was the sole trustee of the Howard Hughes Medical Institute (HHMI), which in turn wholly owned Hughes Aircraft. However, Howard didn't leave a will. Once it was decided that the New Jersey courts would put in place a set of directors for HHMI, we expected the new directors would sell Hughes Aircraft to diversify their assets, which they did in 1985.

General Motors was the highest bidder at $5.5 billion, winning out over Ford Motor Company. Hughes Aircraft Company became General Motors Hughes Electronics, and for the first time ever, we were listed on Wall Street with the letters GMH.

GM Vice Chairman Don Atwood led the acquisition team. I was one of the presenters when the bidders came to Hughes, covering Newport as well as several other operations. Newport was supplying LCD driver chips for the dashboard displays on the new Corvette; fortunately, we were delivering on schedule, which helped make the right impression. Don let it be known he liked my particular presentation.

GM won us in June 1985, but the ownership would not officially take place until year's end. GM's Delco Electronics was to be merged with Hughes Aircraft to form GM Hughes Electronics, which would then report to GM headquarters. I was asked to be on Atwood's fast-start team to see how Hughes and Delco Electronics could profit by working together without waiting for the official transfer of ownership.

Delco wasn't all that happy with the merger. After all, the upward mobility path for most of their executives would still be inside GM, not Hughes Electronics. Given the headstrong characteristics of Hughes engineers, who also possessed minor manufacturing skills compared to Delco's engineers, we may also have been a little tiresome to them. It wasn't long before I realized the "fast start" project could better be called the "slow stall" project. With some exceptions, Delco was doing all they could to slow down the Hughes involvement in Delco's automobile market.

Jack Smith was the CEO and Chairman of GM who made the decision to purchase Hughes in 1985. This Jack Smith was followed, coincidentally, by another Jack Smith (more on him later) who became CEO seven years later. On one trip to Delco in Kokomo, Indiana, I dropped in on the Delco purchasing manager. Used to dealing with suppliers wanting to do business with Delco, he said, "So, Scott, you want to be a supplier to Delco." I retorted, "No, I'm here to figure out why Jack thinks I want to do business with you." This wasn't playing out the way these discussions in his office usually did.

IEG GROUP OFFICE

Adjacent to the Electron Dynamics Division in Torrance, California, Chris had recently built a small group office for the Industrial Electronics Group with a charming atrium surrounded by windowed offices, just right for our needs. In 1987 he was facing mandatory retirement in another year and needed to find his replacement. Chris promoted Jeff Grant, manager of the Electron Dynamics Division, and me, with the title of assistant group executives.

I left Newport with satisfaction. The Solid State Products Division within IEG had grown 17 percent, compounded annually over the nine years I was manager. and now had sales of $100 million a year. We had a modern expanded facility, a good workforce, and competitive technology. Profits were not what I wished, but the balance between Hughes and external markets was about right, with the prime focus on Hughes systems.

Moving to Group, the term used by everybody, I felt the assignment would never surpass the enjoyment and satisfaction of running my own operation, but now Jeff Grant and I had nine profit centers to oversee, a challenge in itself. We worked together smoothly, sharing the responsibilities of the job, learning to run the monthly financial meetings,and getting to better know all of the Industrial Electronics Group's operations. We respected each other and did not let the prospects that one of us would probably get to be president of the group interfere with our work.

The Industrial Electronics Group had a remarkable array of product lines and programs. IEG was on Boeing's new 747-400 with a new level of communication and display systems for each seat passenger not seen before. We had large-screen display systems, such as the one at the stock exchange in Chicago. We were the leading supplier of solar cells for satellites, first in silicon and later using GaAs. We were the leading supplier of small cryo-engines. (Remember the Imaging Infrared Maverick program.)

Hughes in Scotland was growing, with over 1000 employees. They were supplying devices for the UK's belatedly modernized phone system. We had developed SRS, sound retrieval system, which enhanced sound systems for television systems. Sony was the first, paying 50 cents per TV system for SRS. We were the leading company for cathode ray tube (CRT) displays for military and aircraft applications. We dominated the analog medical ultrascan storage and display systems until the changeover to digital systems. For a while, we provided laser material cutting systems for the clothing industry. Our Connecting Devices Division was a dominant supplier of military connectors and was at times the most profitable division in the whole company. The Carlsbad Research Center was providing critical classified sensors to the Star Wars program. I could name a dozen more.

Jeff's Electron Dynamics Division was the leading tube supplier for airborne military radars and satellite transmitters. An Air Force officer once asked Chris why the only transmitter tubes that fail in space come from Hughes. Chris answered, "Because all the tubes in space are from Hughes."

PRESIDENT OF THE INDUSTRIAL PRODUCTS GROUP

By 1988 Dr. Allen Puckett had retired, and Dr. Bud Wheelon, head of the Space Group, replaced Allan as CEO. You may recall our early encounter, when Bud and I disagreed on a new clean room for the research center and I forced a meeting with him in front of Dr. Puckett. Well, now it came time for Chris to retire. Bud selected me to be president of IEG. I was also promoted to corporate vice president, up from group vice president.

I recognized it was going to be hard to top what Chris had achieved, particularly with the U.S. military budget beginning to drop off. I felt we might take more advantage of synergy among the divisions, working together on new products. Until now the divisions were mostly stand-alone operations with little cross-division dependence. To further the idea, I formed an intradivision task team to come up with some good ideas.

I wanted Jeff Grant to stay on with me, but he elected to transfer over to Space Group. Some years later I asked him why he left IEG. He said I was too young, and he didn't want to wait around until I retired. In truth, I did expect to retire from this position. I remember once during one of the many monthly financial reporting sessions quietly doing a little calculation: "Let's see. I'm 53, and I have eleven and a half more years until retirement. . . times 12 months in a year. . . times nine monthly financial presentations. . . .that comes to over twelve hundred more financial meetings before I retire?" How wrong this calculation turned out to be.

SEVENTH INNING BREAK

Let's stop and stretch our legs for a moment; there's a lot more to follow.

It was 1988. I had been at Hughes for 27 years and was very proud of the world's leading military electronics company, with 78,000 employees, and California's largest technology-based company. Either I had adapted to the Hughes style of operating, or I was fortunate that Hughes Aircraft and I naturally had the same way of thinking. Probably a little of both.

Family life was good. Cassie balanced my left-brain way of thinking with her basically different approach to things. I've often said thank God I didn't marry someone like me. Our three sons, Tyler (age 25), Morgan (22), and Brandon (19), were a joy. We never suffered any of the disconnects that sometime happen in a family.

We liked living in southern California, particularly Newport Beach, and had no thoughts of ever living again in the East, where we had grown up. Our health was good. There was much to be thankful for.

The nine major operations in the Industrial Electronics Group had expansions underway. We all loved Christoffers and what he had accomplished. But he was gone, and my responsibility was to keep it going, recognizing the business environment changes, and so must the group.

I was just settling into the task when that proverbial phone rang again.

CHAPTER THREE: 1988–1992

GROUND SYSTEMS

PRESIDENT OF THE GROUND SYSTEMS GROUP

Ground Systems Group (GSG), located in Orange County with headquarters in Fullerton, was one of the five major systems groups in Hughes Electronics. They had 10,000 employees and sales approaching $2 billion per year. They dominated the company's international business.

In the early '80s Ground Systems Group was going strong. They were making good earnings and growing rapidly, but things change. The military began raising serious concerns about product quality. In addition, bookkeeping was getting to be too innovative, people development was lagging, and a number of international programs were disasters. To turn things around, several experienced managers were moved to Fullerton to Ground Systems, led by Blaine Shull. Thanks to Blaine, who was approaching mandatory retirement, and Cal Kirby, another transfer to GSG, the military started to get comfortable with GSG again. John Robert, the CFO at Industrial Electronics Group, was transferred to Fullerton and went to work on the financials. Ground Systems Assistant Group Executive Lou Kurkjian was getting the resources to continue turning operations around. At this same time, I was busy trying to convince Lou to join me in IEG.

Dr. Bud Wheelon, who a year before had named me IEG group president, retired, and Dr. Mal Currie became the CEO of Hughes. Mal needed to pick a new president for Ground Systems, and with supporting recommendations from John, Lou, and Blaine, he asked me to take over. So, I headed back to Hughes systems, something I had left thirteen years earlier when I left missiles systems and never expected to return to. And I was promoted again, this time from a title of corporate vice president to corporate senior vice president. With that, I became the only executive at Hughes to ever start in one group (Missiles), make group president of another group (IEG), and then group president yet again in another group (GSG.)

Although I had overall responsibility, I recognized Lou and another key player, Ken Dahlberg, were far ahead of me in experience in dealing with the U.S. military on Fullerton programs. I felt I could better spend my time mostly working issues inside the plant; they knew how to handle the customers. And to be honest, having worked with the Pentagon before, I didn't really cherish the opportunity to do it again. Before he retired, Blaine took me back to Washington, D.C., and introduced me to the key military officers for Fullerton programs. To me, it seemed that the biggest difference in my working life was that now I was chauffeured up to the riverside entrance to the Pentagon, whereas in my earlier life, I had to walk from south parking.

But we had a number of international programs in serious trouble that no one had their arms around. That had to be addressed.

GROUND SYSTEMS PROGRAMS
NORWEGIAN/DANISH AIR DEFENSE SYSTEM

Before noon on my first day in Fullerton, I was working a major NATO contract to supply Norway and Denmark with an advanced air defense control system that was in very serious trouble. Ground Systems Group had a program to design and install the computers, monitors, and software for a system to control all the military airbases and aircraft in Norway and Denmark. The principal threat for these two countries was a major Russian attack across the northern sector of NATO. The nuclear-hard control rooms were deep inside a mountain in Norway and far below ground in Denmark. There were living quarters for several hundred operators in each center.

The NATO program had been awarded to Ground Systems in 1980. And here we were, 1988, three years late on final delivery, with no operational software. Because of a terrible idea to "stay on schedule," our team had purchased and installed monitors and computers in 1985, stating that all we needed to do now was to supply the software. The computers were of early '80s vintage manufactured in Norway and inadequate for the task. If you want to experience something scary for which you were responsible, visit, as I did some time later, a series of nuclear-hard rooms deep within a mountain reached by a track system suitable for a James Bond movie, or far underground reached by a fast elevator, rooms waiting to become operational for three years. Just sitting there. You would see 100 or so outdated workstations literally just collecting dust plus unoccupied living quarters, all waiting for software from Hughes.

It got worse. One week before I started at Fullerton, the soon-to-be-removed project manager went to Norway to sign a one-more-time, get-well modification to the NATO contract. Now, I had little experience in the development of large software programs, but after Lou and I spent several days reviewing the program, we knew they would fail again, from sheer management incompetence.

The week before Christmas 1988, the Norwegian general responsible for all procurements for the Norwegian Air Force came over to celebrate the newly revised contract. Without any warning, I had to tell him he had just signed a NATO contract that would fail yet again. With a certain distinct tone to his voice, he demanded I be in his office the day after the New Year to say how I was going to fix the program, and I said, "No, I will come over and tell you how we'll go about figuring out how to fix the program."

The general's Danish counterpart was also there for the New Year's meeting in Norway. Front and center, I explained to the crowd that one of the reasons the program was late was that they had in fact changed some of the requirements from time to time, and even now not all of the specs were nailed down. Therefore, in case they were wondering, we would be back to ask for more money. And, of course, we didn't know the new schedule. I still remember my next words exactly: "So, after ten years, we don't know the cost, schedule, or specifications for the program, but other than that everything is on schedule."

I proposed a six-month study phase. I would report back personally every two months. I requested that Norway and Denmark send two experienced officers over to sit with us and report back in parallel. That is exactly what happened. I won't go into all the difficult interplay that took place; let's just say that before this was over, the two generals and I got to know each other pretty well. At one point, Mal Currie, the CEO of Hughes even offered to go to NATO in Brussels and plead that the requirements were beyond state of the art, thereby asking to have the contract cancelled without cause. I told him, "Don't. We are going to fix this thing."

A year or so later, the two generals met with me in my Fullerton office on a Saturday, just the three of us. The objective was to agree on the new funding for a revised program that NATO had once again approved. This hadn't come easy. For example, one NATO country would go along with added funding for the program provided NATO also built them a bridge, for military purposes, of course.

At our meeting that Saturday, the Norwegian general said, "How should we settle on the funding?" I said, "Well, in addition to your funding, so far we have written off a hundred million dollars. It will take us another hundred million to complete the program. So, you owe us two hundred million." He said, "Well, we've already paid you a hundred million, and the loss of efficiencies because of your failures has cost us another hundred million. So, I think, instead, you owe us two hundred million." This is a true story. I said, "Well, it looks like we've got it bounded."

We settled for another $70 million more plus a $2 million incentive to complete on the new schedule. We booked the $2 million. They got a NATO award for the operational system. Over the next several years, we got hundreds of millions more for additional work, including swapping out those old monitors and workstations.

If you read my comment earlier that Imaging IR Maverick was one of two efforts I would care to be remembered for at Hughes, resolving this NATO project successfully is the other.

UKADGE

By 1990 half of the free world was under a defense umbrella designed and build by Hughes Ground Systems Group at Fullerton. Nevertheless, we had still another air defense program in real trouble. It was called UKADGE (United Kingdom Air Defense Ground Equipment). Just as in the case of the program for Norway and Denmark, this program had been underway for a number of years and was badly behind schedule and losing money. This time three major companies were involved: Hughes Aircraft (by now called GM Hughes Electronics) with GE Marconi and Plessy, both in the UK.

The three companies involved in the UKADGE program had formed a corporation called UKSL (United Kingdom Systems Limited). Hughes had the prime software responsibility, while displays and other elements of the project were to come from our two partners. The three companies behaved like subcontractors of UKSL, yet at the same time they owned UKSL. The companies, including Hughes, were not taking overall responsibility for the program.

The UKADGE program was set up to modernize the air defense control system for England and Scotland, replacing an earlier system that was to be scrapped. Our program was five years late, and it appeared we would not deliver before the old system was to be shut down. Prime Minster Margaret Thatcher's administration had recently failed in the development of an airborne radar surveillance system called NIMROD, and now the press and the Labor party were zeroing in on this new Tory embarrassment. As a result Margaret Thacher was getting monthly briefings on the status of our program. As you might imagine, Whitehall (the UK's equivalent of the Pentagon) was very nervous and not very happy with us.

Knowing the program was running late and costing a lot of money, I went to London to sit in on a UKSL board of directors meeting as an observer. The Hughes division manager who reported to me was one of the three board members. During the board meeting, I could see what a mess this organizational relationship had created. No one was really up to the task of simply taking ownership and fixing the program. They were just blaming each other. The three companies needed direction and control from higher management. I found a far more senior executive at GE Marconi who agreed with me. He also helped me see just how much the problem was Hughes's.

The engineers on the program were working at historic Bletchley Park. It was fascinating to visit the historic buildings where Enigma was decoded during World War II. While I was there, one thing caught my eye. The GE Marconi engineers were out the door immediately at closing time, while the Hughes engineers stayed on still working. I learned that the Hughes guys wanted to get this darn program finished and go back home to southern California. On the other hand, the Marconi engineers were in no hurry, as they probably didn't have a job after this project was finished.

I installed a new overall managing director, a feisty Hughes senior project manager, Nancy Price, who had a good track record on major systems. She liked working for Hughes, provided it was outside the United States. I brought more engineers over from southern California for a total of around 50. We set up a fund to give them a performance bonus upon timely completion of the new program schedule and convinced my GE Marconi buddy to do the same for his team. I suspect this was a first for them.

With Marconi on board with my top-down approach to UKSL,

T. Francis Scott, my granddad on my mother's side, about the time I was born. Grandpa and Grandma set the high standards I've tried to live up to.

Dr. Gale H. Walker, my dad, as a young doctor, about the time I was born. Dad became fairly well known nation-wide for his work with mentally deficient children.

W. Scott Walker in 1961, age twenty-six, upon graduation from UVa with a doctorate in nuclear physics. I was heading to Hughes Aircraft Company.

Ted H. Walker, my brother, who was four years older than I, at N.C. State University. He was a graduate student in engineering, 1958.

During high school I drove my jeep fifty miles to Charlotte most weekends to date Cassie, starting just four months after this photo was taken in 1952 when I was seventeen.

All through college and my first year in graduate school, this was my principal means of transportation.

We are off on our honeymoon in Cassie's Buick Roadmaster convertible in 1958, when I was twenty-three.

We were married for the last three years of my graduate schooling. The Rotunda designed by Thomas Jefferson for the University of Virginia is visible in this photo taken on the lawn. Never call it the "campus" at UVa.

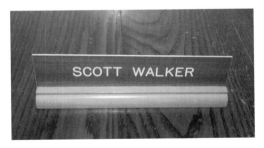

When I started at Hughes, I didn't remember whether I had interviewed as Scott or Bill. They gave me this nameplate for my desk, and with that, I decided to stick with Scott, my middle name.

TYLER'S BOMB

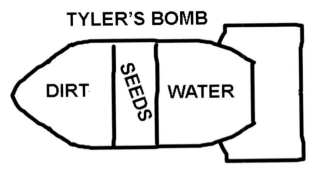

In the middle of the very unpopular Vietnam War, knowing I worked on missiles, young Tyler, about eight at the time, invented this bomb. It breaks open upon impact, disperses seeds into the dirt, and waters the seeds.

In 1973 we moved into our second house, Homewood, built in 1876 by the founder of our town, La Canada Flintridge. It had gas lighting when built and still had some of the gas lines in the walls. The home is well known in the community by its name.

A rare letter from Howard Hughes to General George, the general manager of Hughes Aircraft before the company was split off from Hughes Tool Company in 1955. It calls for both military and civilian products.

Aug. 3, 1949

Dear Gen. George:

I have observed with intense interest and great satisfaction the rapid rise of the Hughes Aircraft Co. in the field of electronics to a position of leadership.

Military applications of electronics are well recognized as of vital importance to the national security. The development of electronic devices of advanced design for military application has been a major factor in our rapid growth.

However, our plans must envisage the research, development and production of electronic devices to fill a very obvious vacuum rapidly becoming apparent in our civilian and industrial economy. In fact, this program is already under way.

Our national security requires the maintenance of world-wide leadership by this country, and I know you and I both feel a very definite responsibility to make even greater and more extensive contributions along the lines of research, development and production of electronic devices both for military and civilian purposes.

Our responsibilities in military work, and our intention to develop civilian products, combine to make for this company a well-rounded program. Our objective must, therefore, be to pursue energetically a vigorous policy to establish this company as the foremost and most progressive electronics producer in this country.

Sincerely,

Howard Hughes

Howard Hughes

The Phoenix AIM 54 (Air Intercept Missile) is shown mounted on a Navy F-14 Tomcat. The 1962 effort at Hughes Aircraft to bid for, and win, the Phoenix missile was my first experience on a proposal team. The missile was called the Phoenix because the Phoenix missile rose from the ashes of an earlier failed missile endeavor by the Navy, just as the mythical Phoenix bird rose from the ashes of its own burned-out nest.

An F-14 is shown with a full load of six AIM 54s which could be launched nearly simultaneously at six enemy aircraft attacking a Carrier Battle Group. The F-14 could stay on patrol station for extended time due to its swing-wing design.

The Imaging Infrared (IIR) Maverick is shown being transported in its storage container with the top lid removed. The missile is twelve inches in diameter and has a shaped-charged warhead designed to penetrate heavily armored tanks. The Imaging Infrared version of Maverick combined with the original TV guided Maverick, provided both day and night capability for the weapon.

A Maverick missile is being launched from an Air Force A-10 Warthog close air support fighter. Both the TV Maverick and the Imaging Infrared Maverick were deployed extensively in Operation Desert Storm.

We went to Disney Studios for comments regarding our innovative design for the new Discovery Science Center in Santa Ana, California, which featured a large black cube mounted on one corner. Disney's key architectural executive said he liked the concept because the design is easy to comprehend at a glance and to remember.

The BBC taped a documentary on AT&T's phone system (red box on the side table) that no longer required re-wiring of offices when moving phone lines. Our Solid State System Division in Newport Beach had one of the early installations.

While we were in Manila, two of my associates and I were invited to go sailing in the South China Seas at the end of the work week. The crew of the 78-foot ketch delighted in hoisting me up in a boson's chair and then dropped me into the water as we sailed on a broad reach.

Michael Hazeltine (in the dark suit), Secretary of State for Defense under Margaret Thatcher, visited Hughes Microelectronics Ltd. in Scotland after the awarding of a defense contract. Ian Duffin, the managing director of HML and I, are greeting Michael during a ceremony with the employees.

Aerial view of the Solid State Products Division in Newport Beach, white buildings, (lower center). Our home is at the far end of the peninsula (upper right corner).

Dr. Ron Finnella, manager of the Carlsbad Research Center, Dick Belardi, assistant division manager in Newport Beach, and I are enjoying an award from the Army for performance on an advanced semiconductor contract.

Ground-breaking for our 100,000-square-foot expansion in Newport Beach. The city mayor is in the middle of the photo. She is between me in a dark suit and Dr. Christoffers, president of the Industrial Electronics Group. The product line managed by Karl Reismuller, (second from the right) would expand into the new building. We also built a five-story parking structure on our eighteen-acre site to handle the increase in employees.

Ribbon-cutting a year later. (left to right) Karl Reissmueller, Scott Walker, and Bill Christoffers.

Ground-breaking in Tijuana, Mexico, for our new maquiladora building. Plant manager Ron Shaver (hatless) is to my left. Karl Reismuller, Assistant Division Manager at Newport Beach, would produce hybrid mirocircuits in the facility. Wearing a blue suit, Karl is looking on from above ground.

Located at the top of Fundadores Boulevard, overlooking downtown Tijuana, our facility named CIRCUITOS DE BAJA CALIFORNIA FUNDADORES (CBT) established a high standard for maquiladores operations. The employees worked in air conditioned, clean rooms with modern computer-based equipment.

I held a press conference that received national coverage to announce a new solvent developed by the Ground Systems Group. The solvent is not harmful to the ozone layer in the upper atmosphere.

To Cassie and Scott Walker
With best wishes, Ronald Reagan

Photo session at the USO celebration after Desert Storm. There were three past Presidents at the event. When we had our picture taken with President Reagan, they noted the color of my tie to insure I was sent the right photo.

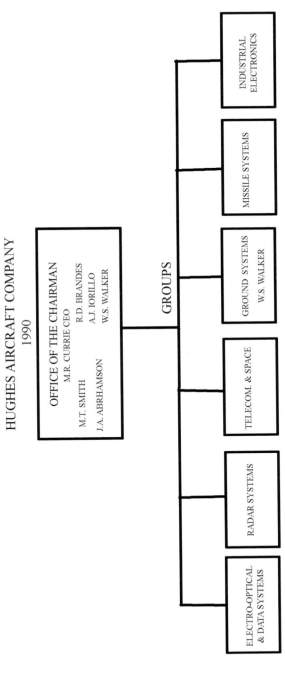

HUGHES AIRCRAFT COMPANY
1990

OFFICE OF THE CHAIRMAN
M.R. CURRIE CEO   R.D. BRANDES
            A.J. IORILLO
M.T. SMITH   W.S. WALKER
J.A. ABRHAMSON

GROUPS

| ELECTRO-OPTICAL & DATA SYSTEMS | RADAR SYSTEMS | TELECOM. & SPACE | GROUND SYSTEMS W.S. WALKER | MISSILE SYSTEMS | INDUSTRIAL ELECTRONICS |

This simplified organizational chart of Hughes Aircraft in 1990 necessarily omits several organizations. The Ground Systems Group had five product divisions and two support divisions, similar to the other Groups. The chart identifies the members of the Office of the Chairman formed by Dr. Currie to help manage the company. I started my career at Hughes in Missile Systems, then moved to the Industrial Electronics Group, and then found myself in the late 80s and early 90s managing the Ground Systems Group with sales approaching $2 billion for the Group.

After the award of the Peace Shield contract for Saudi Arabia, we were hosted before dinner by the nephew of the king at his palace with a showing of his prized hawks. My partner asked if I was to be the next CEO when Dr. Currie retired. I said GM would be going outside for the CEO.

Dinner in the palace. The food was delicious and the conversation engaging. We felt very comfortable and welcomed. Dr. Currie, our CEO, is in the middle of the photo. I am on the right.

After dinner in the palace we adjourned to a large room to watch a video of hunting in North Africa using the hawks I had held on my arm at the reception. I'm seated next to the king's nephew.

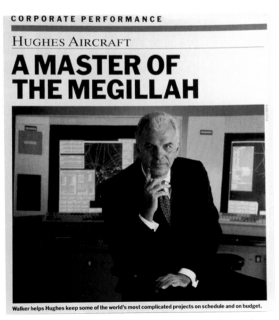

CORPORATE PERFORMANCE

HUGHES AIRCRAFT

A MASTER OF THE MEGILLAH

Walker helps Hughes keep some of the world's most complicated projects on schedule and on budget.

Fortune *magazine (1/27/1992) ran an article about the awarding of the Peace Shield contract for Saudi Arabia air defense, the largest contract ever awarded Ground Systems Group at Hughes Aircraft.*

While she was stationed at San Diego, I was invited aboard the USS La Jolla, *a nuclear powered attack submarine of the Los Angeles class. The submarine's fire control system was built by our Ground Systems Group as were its Mark 48 torpedoes, which were not on board. Nevertheless, while we were submerged, the fire control operator continually established firing solutions on all surface ships in the area. The submarine climbed and dove and banked to turn similar to an airplane's movement, only underwater.*

As good protocol, Cassie and I paid our respects to Chiang Kai Shek at his memorial in Taipei on our first visit.

Sixties night at an offsite meeting of the Business Coalition sponsored by the chancellor of the University of California Irvine. Orange County business executives and selected professors from the university would spend a weekend each year at various offsite locations. That year the event was in Carmel, California, near Route 1, the coastal highway popular with the hippies in the sixties, which perhaps inspired the theme for the costume affair.

Cassie at a dinner in Beverly Hills, at which we hosted a couple from Taiwan. Mrs. Pei Li Bumpas, the Chinese wife of our manager in Taiwan, accompanied our guest to the dinner.

GM HUGHES ELECTRONICS CORPORATION (1995)

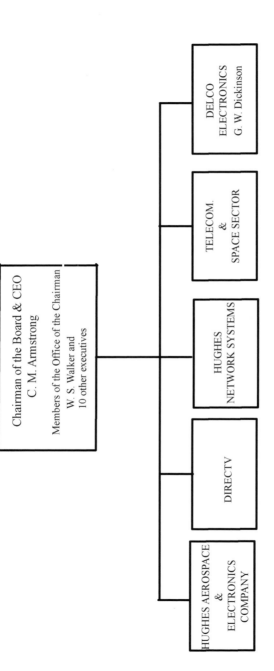

Chairman of the Board & CEO
C. M. Armstrong

Members of the Office of the Chairman

W. S. Walker and
10 other executives

HUGHES AEROSPACE & ELECTRONICS COMPANY

DIRECTV

HUGHES NETWORK SYSTEMS

TELECOM. & SPACE SECTOR

DELCO ELECTRONICS
G. W. Dickinson

By the time I transferred from Hughes Aircraft to Delco Electronics in 1995, the overall Hughes Electronics Company chart showed five major organizations with total sales of around $15 billion. My old Hughes Aircraft Company had been divided into Hughes Aerospace & Electronics Company, the part I had worked in, and three other major organizations: Telecommunications & Space Section, Hughes Network Systems, an acquired company, and now DIRECTV. Moving into Delco Electronics, I would be experiencing an entirely different type of company with its origins in General Motors. Besides being Chief Technology Officer reporting to Gary Dickinson, I still retained my role as a member of the Office of the Chairman with the task of helping integrate Delco and Hughes.

Agreeing to join Delco Electronics as Senior Vice President and Chief Technical Officer, I celebrated at a sushi bar in Tokyo with some Delco employees after a marketing conference.

In the spring of 1996, Cassie and I found a nice home on Geist Lake on the outskirts of Indianapolis. Boating and annual family croquet tournaments were the norm. The drive to my office in Kokomo was over an hour, but I was never late for any of the seemingly unnecessarily early 7 am. meetings.

GM's EV-1, the first production electric vehicle in the U.S. by the major automobile industry, employed key components supplied by Hughes Electronics. We also developed the "Magna-Charger" inductive charging system shown on the left which could safely handle 3 to 25 kilowatts, significantly reducing the time to recharge the batteries.

In 1996 Delco Electronics integrated around twenty features for safety, security, and communication into the SSC concept vehicle, leading the industry in demonstrating electronic functions that are becoming commonplace today. After the two SSC vehicles completed their mission, one was given to Disneyland for display in their Technology of the Future exhibit.

1996
LOUIS SCHWITZER
AWARD

David Schnelker, J Fu Shih
Xing Wu, Ed Rothrock
"Delco Electronics Racing Eye Cue"

On behalf of Delco's Advanced Technology Center, I accepted the Schwitzer award for our "Eye Cue" helmet display system as the best new technology at the 1996 Indy 500 Race.

Delco Electronics had a large infield suite just after Turn Four for the Indy 500 race.

Cassie helped host Regis Philbin as Delco's guest at the Queen's Ball for the race.

In 1997 after retiring, Cassie and I maintained our home in Indiana as our principal residence. At my retirement party, I mentioned my new life would be a "whole new book." Perhaps some day this photo might be in a Book II entitled As I Remember Retirement.

And after Cassie and I had been married fifty years, the Walker family gathered for this photo with our three sons and their families in 2008.

I wanted Plessy corporate to join us, but Plessy was a different animal. They were a smaller outfit than GE or Hughes, and they felt the major problems were not of their making, which may have been mostly true. There was no higher-level Plessy executive in the UK than the division manager, who already was on the UKSL board. Since Plessy had recently been sold to Siemens, headquartered in Munich, Germany, the next higher-up was in Germany.

I had been in London for several weeks in early December working on the various details of the program. The year was 1989, which was a great time to be in Europe, as the Berlin Wall had just fallen. I decided to go to Munich to see if I could get Siemens to play an executive role over Plessy and help take responsibility to fix the project. Cassie was already with me to help host a dinner related to our Norwegian/Danish program. I don't recall why the dinner was in England for a Scandinavian program, but it was. Anyway, we came up with a great idea: we'd have Tyler and Brandon fly over to London, then, for Christmas, we would go to a small hotel Cassie knew about on the coast between Nice and Monaco. On the way down, we would go by Munich so that I could talk with Siemens.

Siemens had recently experienced a dangerous event in which some bad guys had stormed the facility. I believe some executives were killed. Landing in Munich, I took a taxi from the airport directly to the Siemens headquarters. At the main gate, the guard let my taxi driver go on to the headquarters building. The driver commented, "You must be someone important." I asked why. He said, "They always come out to the gate and take the visitor in." This was the first time he had been allowed to drive in. Getting to the executive office, however, still required about three keyed doors and elevators to be opened. I met the German executive and asked him to join GE Marconi and Hughes in our effort to fix the UKSL problems. He said no, that this was strictly a UK problem. Even though Plessy reported to him, I was never able to get Siemens involved.

Cassie, Tyler, Brandon, and I had a fun evening at a Hofbräu in Munich. The next day we flew on to the Mediterranean coast and enjoyed the Christmas holiday in France. Meanwhile, Morgan was already in Europe visiting his girlfriend, who was taking a year in Vienna. The two of them flew down and joined us at our lovely hotel.

And what a classy, small hotel it was. Upon arrival, we were met in the lobby by most of the staff. Ordering at the bar, you didn't need to sign; they knew who you were. Once we took over the lounge and played a game of Monopoly while they served us a light dinner. During a dispute over a rule written in French, Cassie asked the maître d' to read it for us. She came back with her version of what he said and won the game (under protest).

We left Morgan and his girlfriend in Nice on New Year's Eve and flew back to London. That evening Brandon went to Covent Garden to meet a girl he knew. I couldn't help thinking how our sons' college days were so different than mine.

Back to UKADGE. Over the next year, Whitehall wanted program updates every three months. By now I realized the management problems were largely behind us, thanks in large part to Nancy Price. So, every three months I went to London, briefed Whitehall, and enjoyed all the musicals in London's West End.

The program finished on the new schedule, and the team won their performance bonuses. Amazingly, we also ended up receiving a major international award for achievement in military aviation for our work on the IUKADGE. When we transferred the system to UK air force management, Cassie and I hosted a dinner in London for the GE Marconi and Plessy executives along with their wives. I remember my GE partner asking, "Why don't we ever have dinners like this?" They didn't take their wives out to business dinners.

Oh, yes—the girl we left Morgan with on New Year's Eve in the south of France was Ericka, now the mother of three of our grandchildren.

TAIWAN

We had a contract with Taiwan for two large, ground-based radars we couldn't deliver. I had inherited another unhappy international customer, so off to Taiwan I went.

Taiwan was and still is a sort of halfway country, Chinese but not mainland Chinese. During the time I was there, the government was still controlled by Chinese, who had exiled to Taiwan along with Chiang Kai-shek in the late '40s. Amazingly, they seemed to still hold some hope of going back and taking over China, something that will never happen. However, the emerging Taiwanese leaders were born in Taiwan and think differently.

The U.S. was trying to straddle both sides. To appease mainland China, President Carter replaced the State Department and its ambassador to Taiwan with the American Institute. Somehow circular reasoning saves face, as all that happens is career employees from the State Department join the American Institute during their tenure in Taiwan and then rejoin the State Department when they come home. As the new guy from Hughes, I was introduced to the non-ambassadorial head of the American Institute and went through the protocol of a ceremonial visit with my wife to the memorial to Chiang Kai-shek.

Skipping over the details, we finally delivered the first of the two radars. The only problem was it still wasn't working properly. However, Taiwan had taken ownership and had signed the transfer papers. Some of the problems were ours; some of them were due to various deficiencies on the part of the Taiwanese. I offered to take the radar back, which was a great relief to the officers who had signed off on the delivery. We fixed the radar, but now the problem was getting them to sign off again. Doing that made them very nervous.

I remember one formal meeting on the subject, set up in the conventional arrangement with the general and I at the end of a long room with an interpreter behind us to translate, even though this particular general spoke good English. With my guys seated along one wall and the general's guys seated along the opposite wall, I had to suffer through a long diatribe about Hughes. Interestingly, the general interrupted the meeting and said there would be a short break. He took me into his private chambers and in perfect English said, "Relax; this is all for show."

We had programs with all three services, and I came to know a number of high-level Taiwan air force and army generals and navy admirals. I was treated with privilege. When Cassie and I arrived from the U.S., we could bypass customs and go straight to our limousine. I still wear a handsome watch presented to me by a four-star general; there aren't many four-star generals in Taiwan.

It might be worth assessing here the ability of our wives to help us in international business and in which countries. Are the wives of U.S. executives of value in doing business overseas? My experience is as follows: in Norway and Denmark, yes, as exemplified by the fact we still get Christmas cards from the Norwegian general and his wife. In England, as opposed to Scotland, I found few opportunities to bring Cassie into business experiences. To my surprise, in Taiwan Cassie was definitely a lot of help. On a day when I was with the army general who bought our Firefinder radars, Cassie and I were to sponsor an evening dinner for perhaps a dozen officers and their wives. At my meeting with the general that afternoon, he apologetically announced he would not be able to attend, as the Taiwan president was hosting a Latin American president that evening, and he was expected to attend.

Meanwhile, his wife, my wife, the Chinese wife of our resident Hughes manager, and several other ladies of high-ranking officers were having a luncheon, holding hands and singing Christian songs. Cassie was doing what she does so graciously. That evening at our dinner, the general walked in. I looked at him, and he just shrugged his shoulders and said, "My wife said we are going to the Walkers' dinner, not the other dinner."

SOME INTERNATIONAL SHORT STORIES
Once I paid a visit to Portugal on the matter of a radar unit we had delivered and also to gather some market information for a new program, for which we subsequently did not bid. Cassie had her Hasselblad camera case stolen out of our car on that trip, but the thieves had failed to grab the camera case which was next to the camera. She had already taken a charming photo of old-town Lisbon.

Lou Kurkjian and I divided up the international program, with one of his being a project for Egypt. Since Egyptian officers were quartered in Fullerton for several years, Lou put in a prayer room for their use. When the prayer rug was stolen, Lou put down another rug, but not until the direction to Mecca was officially specified. Over a lunch, I asked a young Egyptian officer, who had been in California for two years, whether they were speaking in Arabic to their young child. He said they tried, but their daughter said, "Daddy, I don't speak Spanish." "It's time for you to go home," I told him. Our program with Egypt resulted in Lou's having a pleasant exchange with President Mubarak of Egypt.

During Desert Storm, we happened to have a field engineer in

Jordan under U.S. Army contract. I pulled him back home over the objections of our Army. I didn't know whether Jordan was going to side with us or with Iraq, and I didn't much care what the Army wanted. We weren't going in-country to get our man back, as Ross Perot once did for Electronic Data Systems employees in Iran. I talked with our guy when he got back to California, and he said, "Thanks. You made the right decision."

With U.S. government approval, China tried to purchase one Firefinder II, an advance version of our enemy-projectile detection and tracking system, which we were selling to Taiwan. I resisted, saying, "Yeah, they will buy one all right, tear it apart, and then start building them for themselves."

CANADIAN AIR TRAFFIC CONTROL

Well, enough about past international programs. Let's get on to my own start-up international programs. Air traffic control systems and air defense control systems are sometimes thought of as the same thing in reverse. Air traffic control uses radar to direct a plane down to the earth. Air defense control uses radar to direct a plane up from the earth.

The Federal Aviation Administration (FAA) had Hughes Ground Systems and IBM under a study contract for a next-generation air traffic control system. At Ground Systems Group, the combined investment by the government and Hughes came to fifty million dollars. Just before I arrived in Fullerton, IBM won the U.S. program, which was a bitter loss for GSG.

Now it was Canada's turn to update their air control system across the entire country, plus the oceanic segments off each coast. During my first year at Fullerton, I had to make the decision whether we should spend the sizable resources over the next year to compete again. Obviously IBM would be a strong contender for the Canadian system. I called Mal Currie, our Canadian-born CEO, for his opinion. He said, "Yes, go ahead and bid, but only if you can win." Some help that was; if I knew we would win, I wouldn't have called.

I decided to go for it. My reasoning was rather simple. We spent $50 million on air traffic control and lost. Yet, we only went to bat once. It seemed to me that for $50 million you should give the batter at least two times at bat. Hughes and IBM both submitted proposals.

There were three factors involved for winning in Canada. It turned out both companies' proposals were technically acceptable. That's one down, a tie. Both proposals came in around $500 million with a difference of only $5 million, not a significant factor. That's two down, still a tie.

The third factor was the "economic benefits" proposal. The Canadian position was that if they were sending all this money outside of their country, they should expect we would do something in exchange that would benefit Canada. And they weren't bashful. They expected an economic benefits package of about the same magnitude as the contract they would give out.

This meant putting five hundred million dollars' worth of business into Canada. To do that, we formed Hughes Canada Limited. I was on the board of directors, with Mal as the chairman. He took the overall lead on finding businesses we could put in Canada. If we won, I would put most of our program work in Canada, moving a number of southern California engineers above the border. We moved several small commercial subsidiaries to Canada. IBM did about the same, using whatever resources were natural for them. They were aware of the size of the economic package expected, just as we were, perhaps another tie.

However, the Canadians had a criterion that wasn't in writing. They had a preconceived preference for certain provinces they wished to benefit most from this economic package and hadn't stated what provinces they favored. IBM bet on Ontario and Quebec, the industrial eastern provinces, and set up their benefit packages there. Our marketing team figured out early that Parliament wanted this program to benefit the western region. So we announced we would put the program office in British Columbia, and our small start-up companies would be in Alberta and Saskatchewan, three western provinces. By the time IBM figured out that the western provinces were supposed to benefit the most, it was too late. They couldn't turn their ship around in time. We won the Canadian air traffic control program.

By the way, the person put in charge up in Vancouver, British Columbia, after two earlier project managers failed at the task was Nancy Price, our gal who had finished the task in the UK and liked to work in foreign countries.

SAUDI ARABIA

Hughes is not the only company that on occasion had trouble delivering on large software projects. Boeing had an air control program with Saudi Arabia called Peace Shield, which was contracted through the U.S. Air Force. It was supposed to be in operation before Operation Desert Storm. As was generally known, Boeing was on the verge of being terminated. I visited the colonel in charge at Hanscom Field, Massachusetts, offering to provide Boeing some software help because: one, Boeing was a friend of Hughes Aircraft; two, the U.S. Air Force, another of our friends, was in an awkward position with the Saudis; and three, it got our nose under the tent. We placed a couple of software engineers at Boeing, but it wasn't long until the Air Force terminated Boeing for cause.

The Air Force then ran a new competition for Peace Shield. Westinghouse would be our principal competitor. The way the program worked, the Saudi air force contracted with the U.S. Air Force, who, in turn, contracted with the U.S. supplier.

Now that you're familiar with "economic benefit" packages, it might not surprise you that this program also had one, with several big differences. First, there was no mention of an "economic benefit" package in the U.S. request for proposals. After all, our contract would be with the U.S. government, not Saudi Arabia. At first I suggested we just wouldn't offer an economic package. I was told that idea won't work; you just had to know they wanted a package. I still wonder what would have happened if we had said no to an economic benefit package and at the same time the U.S. selected our proposal over Westinghouse.

The second problem was how do you make it work over there? You would have to bring in the technology, you would bring in the material to be assembled, and you would likely even bring in the workforce to do the work. And where do you sell it? You would have to export it to markets elsewhere. Under these circumstances, just where was the added value for us while in Saudi Arabia?

Mal Curie, our CEO, who was soon to retire, Lou Kurkjian, the assistant group executive, Dick Brandes, another Hughes executive, and I were invited to an affair at a palace on the outskirts of Riyadh, sponsored by a nephew of King Fahd. The evening started with Shirley Temple cocktails in a large tented area. I sat next to the lead air force general who asked if I was going to be the next CEO of Hughes. I had to say no, and furthermore, GM would be going outside the company for the next CEO. After the so-called cocktail affair, the host showed off his prize hawks by placing them on stands with hoods over their heads. They allowed me to hold one on my leather-covered arm. The hawks are both heavy and very expensive.

When it was time for dinner, we passed by a large walled-in building, which was the women's quarters. In the several homes I visited in Riyadh, I never saw any females, nor did I expect to. Our host was allowed four wives and as many concubines as he could afford. Being the nephew of the king, I wondered how many that would be. As we entered the main palace, men were spraying incense into the air. We washed our hands and sat down on the floor for a very enjoyable dinner, particularly if you liked camel's milk.

After dinner, our host ushered us into a large sitting room to watch a video of his recent hunting trip in North Africa. As best as I could make out from the video, hunting consisted of our friend sitting on a chair in the back of a large truck and taking off the hawk's hood at the appropriate time. The whole evening was a delight, as they were very cordial and made us feel quite comfortable.

My hawk-hunting friend also was a diabetic and had a foundation to help people around the world who were becoming blind from the disease. Once, while he was staying at the Beverly Wilshire hotel, I was invited to have a private dinner with him at the hotel. I decided to stay overnight, and the hotel was well prepared for my arrival. I don't know how many people were traveling with him, but it seemed like he took over an entire floor.

While in Kingdom, we visited several radar sites that were to be incorporated in the air defense system, including one very high up on a mountain. The radar was not located in the most obvious place. When I asked why they put the radar "over there" when "over here" would be more advantageous, someone explained my choice was where they set the fires that direct pilgrims across the desert going to Mecca.

On another occasion, Mal set up a dinner with the Marine general who led the famous "Left Hook" desert tank drive across the Arabian desert that took the Iraqis by surprise during Operation Desert Storm. This was the largest tank maneuver since General Patton's days. I just knew the general would start moving the salt and pepper shakers and whatever around the dinner table to lay out the progress of the attack, and sure enough he did. The general interviewed a captured Iraqi general during the attack, who said, "You weren't supposed to come in over here; you were supposed to come in over there!"

GPS was not yet in the military inventory for tanks, so the general had his tank navigator buy a commercial one from an advertisement in a magazine. After his navigator said he had it figured out, they used it to keep from getting lost going across the barren desert during the Left Hook attack.

We won the Peace Shield competition over Westinghouse and Unisys for $800 million. As for the economic benefits package, we set up a corporation headed by our CEO to handle the task. I was on the board of directors.

And no, there weren't any opportunities for Cassie to help in the Kingdom. But you may enjoy the following. At Fullerton I had a crackerjack contracts gal. If this was a usual U.S. program, it would have simply been her turn to do the contract work. She approached me and asked to have the opportunity to take on the Saudi challenge. I gave her a small booklet on the social cultures and mores of Saudi Arabia. She read it and said she still wanted to try. So I gave the program to her, and she handled herself fine in Kingdom. The local women in Riyadh had to wear burkas, but she could show her face, keeping her hair under a scarf and a black smock over her clothes. When she came back from one of her trips, I asked her how it went dealing with the Saudis. I loved her answer: "They didn't know how to handle a woman, so I ran all over them."

Fortune magazine carried an article about our Peace Shield win. The headline was "A Master of the Megillah." Using megillah, a Yiddish term meaning "a complicated matter," seemed a poor choice of words for a story involving Saudi Arabia. Otherwise, I liked the article, which gave us more credit than we deserved for performance on large complex software programs.

Winning Peace Shield and the subsequent successful performance should be credited to the contributions of a number of Hughes people, particularly Lou Kurkjian, my closest partner, Chuck Sutherland, the program manager and others deserving as much or more credit than I. As subsequent chapters in this book discuss, I moved on to other matters after helping to win Peace Shield, the largest contract Ground Systems ever had.

There was one last contribution to the program that I would like to mention, because it speaks so well of Hughes. As I can best remember, the contract called for 54 months for completion with a penalty of around $50 million for being as much as three months late and a bonus of the same amount for completion three months early. We went for the $50 million bonus with a vengeance. I was successful in getting corporate to settle 50/50 on any bonus award. Up to $25 million would be divided by a formula for the team performing on the contract, from the program manager to the secretaries and everyone else. Hughes would take as profit the other $25 million. Then in my last visit to the Kingdom during a review of the program, the Saudi presenter showed the 54-month schedule for which they had tasks to complete so that we could install our part in the last year. I reminded them in no uncertain terms that our working schedule had us delivering three months early so as to receive the full bonus, and they should perform their tasks to the same schedule, that is, shortened. "If we are ready to come in Kingdom and can't perform because you are off the shortened schedule, we will be asking for the bonus anyway." As I mentioned, I left before contract completion, but as I remember, we got the full bonus.

MARK 48 ADCAP TORPEDO

A key program for us in the early '90s was the ADCAP (ADvanced CAPability) Mark 48 torpedo. It was the most advanced torpedo in the Navy's arsenal and probably still is. Before my time at Fullerton, GSG had established a plant in Jackson, Mississippi, for production of the Mark 48 torpedo. Why Jackson, Mississippi? Well, they had a good labor force to draw from, and not by coincidence, the district held an important seat in Congress. To get the support of the local community, I got involved with the local interests and in particular Jackson University, a traditionally black college, which proved to be a personally rewarding experience.

The Navy decided to have its two suppliers, Westinghouse and Hughes, compete for a winner-take-all for the remaining production years. This was one of five must-win U.S. military programs I had established.

As I think of the ADCAP program, I would like to add a note or two regarding Pat Hyland. Although Pat Hyland retired nine years before the ADCAP procurement and was at this time 92 years old, he was still following activities at Hughes. During the ADCAP proposal effort, Pat called me to say he was concerned about our chances of winning, as Westinghouse was the Navy's sole source for the key sensor in the torpedo. I agreed that I didn't like the cards we were holding, but went on to explain our game plan, noting the Navy was making the sensor available to Hughes. He said he just wanted to be sure I was thinking. Two weeks later he passed on.

A couple of other fond memories for this man: out of respect for him everyone at Hughes always addressed him as Mr. Hyland. For some reason I always called him Pat. He never seemed to mind. I note that when he published his autobiography, he chose to title the book *Call Me Pat*. Guess he really did like to be called by his first name. The subtitle of the book was *The Autobiography of the Man Howard Hughes Chose to Lead Hughes Aircraft.*

Earlier, Pat Hyland had paid me a visit in Newport Beach after visiting NEC semiconductor operations in Japan. He wanted to tell me what he learned and thought I should pay them a visit, which I eventually did. During my meeting with Pat, I offered him a nice Lucite-encased display of our various crystal oscillators and crystal filters. He said, "Oh, don't throw pearls before swine; I have retired." I commented, "Yes, but I note you still head the financial committee of the board of directors. And Pat, I learned when I had financial responsibility for advanced development of new air-to-surace missiles several years ago that controlling the money is all the control you need." He just smiled.

And one last remembrance: when I took over Ground Systems Group in 1988, he arranged to have a lunch with my two associates, Lou Kurkjiam and John Roberts and me in a private dining room on the

Queen Mary in Long Beach. Pat was particularly close to the Ground Systems Group and wanted to give us some useful advice, which he did. I believe that was the last time I saw Pat.

We won the ADCAP production contract Pat had been concerned about. The ADCAP was one of the must-win key U.S. military contracts that year. We also won the other four must-win programs.

LITTLE RECOGNITION FOR NOT DOING SOMETHING

On occasion I've made the observation that not doing something was the right action, even though the very nature of not doing something passes by unrecognized. If a mistake is avoided, life goes on with little notice. It is only when the mistake is not avoided that there is plenty of recognition. Thinking back, I can remember a number of instances.

As the need to clean up contaminated land areas around the country increased, there were numerous business opportunities. A well-meaning crew at GSG wanted to get involved with a major river contamination cleanup in the northeast. We would have overall management responsibility, and the team was rather excited. Well, we had no particular experience in the earth-moving technology required, let alone the delicate political and liability issues involved. The team had already gotten their feet in the water (excuse the analogy) when it came to my attention. I stopped them cold. I believe we could easily have gotten into some very serious complications on a project that is still controversial twenty years later.

I'll give just another example to make the point. From a physics standpoint, the superconducting supercollider (SSC) was a very exciting project. It was to be a particle accelerator 54 miles in circumference to be built in an area south of Dallas, Texas. I was approached by the team leaders asking if we would care to manage major aspects of the project. By one measure, this would be quite a feather in our cap, while at the same time drawing heavily on our management skills, which were perhaps already thin. Also, we were almost totally unskilled in big physics. I thanked them for the offer and turned them down. Construction for the intended $4.4 billion project got underway and was terminated a few years later when it had grown to over $12 billion and still counting. How glad I am we didn't loose focus on our prime missions by getting involved.

I realize you can't prove a negative, but sometimes looking back I feel many of these decisions not to do something were some of my better accomplishments.

OPERATIONS

FIVE AND FIVE PROGRAM

I heard from our human resources department that some of our African American and Latino employees would like to form support groups. That certainly was all right with me, since I had supported similar activities in IEG, but I learned that several of the Fullerton employees were nervous that if they wanted to meet in this way, Ground Systems Group management might single them out as disruptive activists. This feeling was left over from the behavior of an earlier misguided executive, so I went out of my way to reassure them that the present situation was just the opposite. We encouraged the support groups, typically meeting at lunch, maybe once a week, and I attended several meetings of each group.

Collectively, we came up with an idea that I think was forward-looking. The groups went to local high schools to ask the principals to recommend promising, talented students graduating that year. The key added criterion was that the ones we wished to select would be kids not planning to go to college that year for whatever reason, in spite of their promising talent. They would learn real-world skills by working with mentors in our company. The school principals were quite excited about the program.

On their own, the two support groups selected five African Americans and five Latinos from the candidate list; hence the program became known as the Five and Five Program. The students were offered one-year assured jobs at GSG, which would be paid for at the group level with no direct charges to the departments the students joined. Each of the ten young employees was given a mentor, a volunteer from the two support groups. They might work in shipping, run errands, or handle simple tasks, depending on their skills and the needs of the various departments in which they were placed.

The program came off fairly smoothly. I particularly remember one young African American girl who was brilliant, liked to write poetry, and lived in a one-room apartment with her mother and father, both on drugs. She wanted to go to college but had no wherewithal. She successfully completed our program. Some did go on to college with good skills and experience. Also, I heard from a number of the mentors how much they enjoyed the opportunity to help the students. Several said they realized they should be providing better support to their own children.

I planned to continue the program with another set of students the following year, but alas, the whole company was going into a net layoff position. Predictably, some of our employees, concerned for their own jobs, felt we would be hiring the students while putting their jobs at risk. I doubted that would have happen, but I had little choice but to drop the Five and Five program after one year.

THE COALITION OF CONCERNED BUSINESSES

In the early '90s, the state of California and the state air quality board became increasingly aggressive, demanding businesses reduce the number of cars used to get their employees to work. We were forced to require a certain number of employees to carpool. The number of cars in our parking lots was counted to get an estimate; I think they wanted an average like 0.7 cars per employee. I invited the head of the state air quality board to come pay a visit. Over lunch, we had a friendly intellectual debate.

One of my arguments was that the cause of the poor air quality was due to the well-known effect of the inversion layer over the LA basin. This, I contended, was compounded by the natural extended dimensions of southern California, with businesses widely distributed, not centralized. This in turn encouraged a broad scattering of housing and the extensive use of automobiles. And none of this was the fault of the business I represent. "So why are you punishing us for something that wasn't caused by us?" His retort was at least honest: "Because we can." Several days later, I got a call saying how refreshing it was to have had such a good debate. I guess so. Net result, we underwrote the leases on vans for a number of our employees to carpool. They were to pay us back via carpool fees they placed on themselves.

This same level of aggressiveness by the state led to the hopelessly-too-early requirement that seven percent of the new cars sold by the major auto companies in the year 2000 must be zero emission, which means pure electric vehicles. This state regulation caused GM to start the EV-1 program, an electric car project. The EV-1 program will come up again in this report.

The businesses in Orange County also had their initiatives. Bob Fluor of Fluor Industries formed what was called the Coalition of Concerned Orange County Businesses to help raise money to improve the traffic situation. Our goal was not so much improving air quality as simply getting our employees to work and home faster and improving the general quality of living in our county. I joined the coalition.

An Orange County bond issue to raise taxes to be put towards improving the traffic situation was put before the public. Immediately, it was attacked by the local Libertarian newspaper, which took the position that we were just pawns of the real estate owners wanting the citizens to pay for roads for their developments. Thanks in part to the newspaper's aggressive attacks, the bond issue failed. In fact Orange County had never voted for any bond on any issue. The following year, a similar transportation bond issue for Orange County failed again, with the same newspaper coming out strong against the measure.

Then, the following year, Bob Fluor passed away, and I was asked to head the coalition. We went for the transportation bond a third time. I should note that "we" is more than the Coalition of Concerned Orange County Businesses, and I would give the others credit if I could remember who they were. Anyway, I decided to take on the *Register* newspaper head to head and asked Disneyland and the telephone company to join me for a meeting with the editor of the newspaper. Combined, the three companies represented a sizable portion of Orange County employees. Between GSG and my old IEG, Hughes alone was the third-largest employer in Orange County.

Our meeting with the newspaper was energetic. First, I insisted that I represented 18,000 Hughes employees and not the real estate developers, and the same went for the other two companies in attendance. Second, I said I did not know how to fix or even improve the traffic situation in Orange County, but I did know the solution required expenditure of money. So, the immediate question was how to generate the funds. Back and forth we went, with the Libertarian coming up with some ridiculous alternatives.

The paper certainly didn't support us, but this time they didn't attack us either. We won a half-cent sales tax to be added in Orange County for the next twenty years. We formed an oversight committee to make sure the money was really spent on transportation and added as big a "moat" around the money as we could. There are many positive results. Perhaps the best known is the flyover-carpool-lane at the interchange of the I-5 and the "55."

You may remember that Orange County went bankrupt in a subsequent year. The county commissioners started looking around for money. By then, the transportation tax had built up a kitty of about $500 million, which was being held until a transportation task force was ready for it. Boy, did the county commissioners ever try to get their hands on it, even going to the state to get them to override the moat we had placed around the bond money. They failed.

OPERA PACIFIC

Since I was the senior executive of Hughes who lived in Orange County, I was frequently called upon by the company to handle Orange County civic responsibilities. I once got a call from our corporate president asking if I liked opera. "Well, maybe. What's up?" Don Atwood, the vice chairman of GM, was an opera buff. Furthermore, the director of the Detroit opera had taken on the additional position of managing director of Opera Pacific in Orange County. I ended up on the board of Opera Pacific, with lots of opening nights, black ties, beautiful new gowns, and receptions with prima donnas.

In my opinion, a typical opera really has only about 30 minutes at best of great singing; the rest is, well, stuff in between great arias. A four-night performance costs about $2 million, half paid for with tickets and half by companies like Hughes and rich opera buffs. I had lunch with the managing director and asked him, "Why can't we hear good opera without it costing so much?" Answer: "You want great singers, it takes money. Money means large theatres. Large theatres are hard to fill, so you end up with $2 million per opera, with at best tickets covering only half that cost." Guess that is just the way it is. We did our part.

DISCOVERY SCIENCE CENTER

A group in Orange County wanted to start a discovery science center, and I was asked to be on the board of directors. I was rather excited, thinking I would have the opportunity to help come up with some exhibits. Wrong. They just wanted Hughes money.

Before locating a major contributor who would get to put their name on the Discovery Science Center, we wanted to be sure our rather unusual architectural design was good. So, the head of our board, our architect, Peggy Goldwater (daughter of Barry Goldwater), and I visited the gentleman at Disney Studios who had overall responsibilities for the design of Disney buildings to get his opinion on the design. He occupied Walt Disney's old office in a wooden two-story building in Burbank, while Mike Eisner, the CEO, was in the adjacent new high-rise building.

The proposed design for the Discovery Science Center was essentially a large cube perched on one point. The Disney executive really liked the design and said he wished they had come up with it first. Today, the Discovery Science Center is a big cube perched on that envisioned point and is visible while driving through Santa Ana on the I-5. And who ended up as the major sponsor with their name on the building? Well, the center was called the Taco Bell Discovery Science Center. Guess I had wished for something a little higher scale. As I write this in 2010 I see the Discovery Science Center has dropped the Taco Bell name from its title. Still, I am glad to acknowledge the help they gave in getting the Center underway with early funding.

As I drove into Disney Studios in a new Cadillac for our meeting with the Disney executive, the guard stopped me for identification. I had just acquired a new personal license plate with the words "HK MATTA," popularized by the successful Disney movie *The Lion King*. Adding the rest of the letters in the phrase, it becomes "Hakuna Matata," meaning "No more troubles for the rest of your days." The guard spotted it immediately and asked if I had worked on *The Lion King*. I couldn't resist the opportunity and answered, "How do you think I got this new Cadillac?" He let me in.

BOY SCOUTS

Another call came in, this time asking us to host a luncheon to raise funds for the Boy Scouts in Orange County. I was to identify a deserving business person and sponsor him as the speaker, with contributions to come from the local business community. I picked a successful retired local businessman who had agreed to take a very responsible job in the Clinton administration even though he was a Republican. I thought he deserved credit simply because the President of the United States asked him to serve his country, and he agreed to be the luncheon speaker. He surely didn't need the money when he went to Washington.

I had a dickens of a time raising the contribution: the goal was $50,000, the same amount that was achieved the year before by someone else. But many Orange Country heavy hitters were turning me down. Finally, someone told me the Lincoln Club (read right-wing Republican) voted not to support the luncheon because the fellow had gone over to work for Clinton, a Democrat. We raised $30,000, and I learned that politics isn't a bean-bag game, Boy Scouts or no Boy Scouts.

THE RUSSIANS ARE COMING, THE RUSSIANS ARE COMING

After the collapse of the Soviet Union, the State Department, with concurrence from the Department of Defense, allowed a Russian visit to Hughes Electronics, and somehow Ground Systems Group was asked to play host. About thirty "scientists" were in their party; I suspected half were KGB types. We gave them a series of briefings on air traffic control and other unclassified programs.

Whenever we had visitors from foreign countries, we always ran their country flag up the flagpole. While the talks were going on, I went down to the entrance to take a look. I had never imagined I'd see the day the Russian flag would be flying in front of my office building. However, outside the lobby, the U.S. flag was up instead. When I enquired of the guard in the lobby, a retired Marine, he said, "I put it up when they came in, and I'll put it up again when they leave, but that's it."

After the Russians left, we mapped out every place they had been, including the restrooms, and did a sweep of all the locations but didn't find any bugs. That evening, we hosted a cocktail party for the Russians at the Disneyland hotel. One of the Russians noted, "You seem afraid of us. Why?" I said it would just take time. I never did really understand why the company put me through all of this

HELICOPTER PERK

If you were to ask a Hughes executive to name a perk he or she was going to miss the most when retirement came, having use of our helicopters to get around the LA basin and surrounding areas would rate near the top. There was a heliport on the roof of my office building and a landing pad adjacent to the corporate building in Culver City. Arguably, one could justify the expense of calling up a helicopter to transit to corporate and back because going by car would pretty much take up the whole afternoon. Instead, I could leave my office half an hour before a meeting at corporate, caucus onboard on the way there, and do it again on the way back to my office. I believe our two helicopters were some version of the six-passenger, two-engine Sikorsky S-76.

SAVING THE OZONE LAYER

Just as other military electronics companies, we used a lot of solvents to clean our products to strict military specifications. The solvents, however, contain chlorine, which contributed significantly to the depletion of the ozone layer in the stratosphere. A clear alternative was not at hand. An engineer at Fullerton started experimenting with lemon juice at home in his kitchen, and eventually he formulated an alternative solvent that got military approval. Not being in the solvent business, I directed the team to license interested companies to manufacture and distribute the new liquid solvent. To launch the product we held a press conference in the corporate lobby.

With the best delivery style I could muster, I tried to explain it all to the local and national press in attendance. Since I'm a supporter of UC Irvine, I also took the opportunity to mention Professor Frank Sherwood Rowland, who won the Nobel Prize for discovering ozone-depleting effects of chlorine. But when the press learned that an old timer of an electronics engineer at Hughes, Ray Turner, had developed the new solvent starting in his kitchen, he became the focus of attention, and most of the questions were directed to him, which pleased both him and me. CNN *Headline News* followed up on the press release in short order. Hughes PR sent some B-video (background video of Hughes Aircraft) to Atlanta, they added some graphics, and in less than one hour, it was on the national news. Amazing.

Right after the presentation, a reporter from a local news station asked me how long chlorine would remain in the upper atmosphere and deplete the ozone. I really had no idea, but to emphasize the problem, I said, "Oh, maybe 200 years." That evening the newscaster in an all-knowing voice explained how the chlorine would remain in the ozone layer for 200 years. I wonder if he was close to being right.

CHAPTER FOUR: 1992–1994

CORPORATE OFFICE

A NEW ERA

COMMERCIAL ENTERPRISES

The day the Berlin wall came down, November 9, 1989, is as good a date as any for the start of a new era for Hughes as well as for the whole world. With military sales dropping off after ten years, our CEO, Mal Currie, launched an initiative for new commercial enterprises. Following corporate lead, at Fullerton we encouraged our divisions to come forth with new ideas. Lou, John, and I would reserve Friday lunch in our private dining room for engineers to give us briefings on their suggestions.

One successful commercial enterprise was a poor man's terminal air-control system. With eastern European air travel starting to open up, their airfields had a critical need for better terminal air-control systems. We sold a number of low-cost systems that could work alongside outdated Russian radars at cities once behind the Iron Curtain.

We also were an early developer of toll road traffic-control systems, installing a pay system in Toronto, Canada. We had a related system that allowed 18-wheelers to bypass highway weigh stations after being cleared upstream. We developed a sensor-based control system to allow Bay Area Rapid Transit (BART) in San Francisco to increase its rush-hour capacity.

One of the commercial enterprises included in our Canadian economic benefit effort was a sound-processing system to test rotating parts for subtle defects while in a noise environment. The product, used to screen alternators during manufacture for GM and Toyota, was derived from our Navy shipboard and submarine sonar systems.

There were several other endeavors, but none of the Fullerton efforts was able to define a new commercial base for Hughes Electronics. The Space Group did achieve the objective: it was called DirecTV.

A CALL FOR REORGANIZATION

In 1989, before going on vacation over the year-end holiday, Mal asked six of us to suggest ways to reorganize the company. The groups were always stand-alone operations, and this was going to change. Our family, along with Steve Jobs, spent Christmas at the small, secluded Kona Village on the big island of Hawaii. I remember preparing myself for the new world that would soon begin for Hughes. A key phrase going through my mind was, "Pack light for the new journey."

By the time our study task was over and changes were starting to be put in place, I had two offices. For awhile at least, I still had my group president's office in Fullerton, but now I had an additional office in the corporate building in Culver City. Most of the day-to-day operations out in Fullerton were handled by Lou Kurkjian. Correctly, I felt I would never be back at Fullerton.

My new secretary at corporate had been Pat Hyland's secretary during his retirement years. Since I needed some office furniture, she mentioned that Pat's rather modest and well-worn desk and swivel chair were in storage and wondered if I would like to have them. It was a treat to sit behind a desk that was so familiar from the other side for over 25 years. When I vacated my office in the corporate building, another executive quickly took over Hyland's desk and chair.

Mal formed the "Office of the Chairman," and I became one of its members. We met weekly and worked on various top-level change issues. For example, we discussed our employee benefits package, which was pretty darn good, but was designed in an earlier era. The corporate human resources manager characterized it as designed for a family with the husband working at Hughes and the wife running the house with two children at home. He said that might represent only 30 percent of our employees in the present day. We changed to a smorgasbord package in which the employee picks and chooses the benefits that best suit his or her situation.

A NEW CEO

Mal, like the rest of us if we are fortunate to turn 65, had to retire. He wanted to stay on a little while longer to help redefine the company, but the GM board of directors refused his request. I teased him, "It was your mother's fault. She should have given birth to you a year later; then you could have stayed around another year."

It was not a surprise that after forty years, the next CEO came from outside of Hughes. When Mike Armstrong, a senior executive at IBM, realized he would not become CEO at IBM, he made himself available for the position at Hughes. In addition to heading Hughes Electronics, GM placed him on GM's highest-level operational committee, so now we had a direct voice at the top of the parent company. This would be the first time I was not reporting up through a line of engineers or scientists, most with a Ph.D. Mike was not slow at setting up his own style of management, which held executives very accountable.

There was an overall workforce reduction of 10,000, which was done with considerable sensitivity. People within five years of retirement were given prorated retirement benefits. When it was feasible, people were given a three-month period to relocate within the company to other positions that still might be open. In general, during this end-of-the-Cold-War economic downturn, Hughes Electronics dealt with the unpleasant task in a fine manner.

AEROSPACE AND DEFENSE SECTOR

In the first year, 1992, we reorganized the six old groups into sectors. A portion of my old Ground Systems Group, along with the Radar Group and the Electro-Optical Group and two subsidiaries, Hughes Santa Barbara and Delco Santa Barbara, were all integrated into the $5 billion Aerospace and Defense Sector with combined sales of $5 billion. The entire company, including Delco Electronics,was $15 billion.

Dick Brandes was named president of the Aerospace and Defense Sector. I was named assistant executive of the Aerospace and Defense Sector and continued as senior vice president and member of the Office of the Chairman.

Dick and I divided up the various oversight responsibilities. I was already quite familiar with most of the programs within our integrated Aerospace and Defense Sector. Thinking back over this period of time, with the exception of Delco Santa Barbara, which I will discuss in a moment, not much of a new nature comes to mind. The focus was on steady performance, reducing redundancies within our new sector, and making our financial targets. I do remember that we did make our numbers, however.

DELCO SANTA BARBARA

I oversaw Delco Santa Barbara while Dick Brandes took Hughes Santa Barbara. The two operations were located essentially across the highway from each other just north of Santa Barbara. Delco Santa Barbara, which was transferred into our sector from Delco Electronics, was a natural fit, with military systems being their core market. I particularly enjoyed working with this new addition to Hughes, as their products were new to me, and I found myself playing a strong role, integrating them into the rest of Hughes.

The origin of Delco Santa Barbara went back to 1959, when GM purchased Dynatrol Corporation, founded by Don Atwood. Don joined GM and had a very successful career, ending as vice chairman of the company. You may recall that Don led the acquisition effort when GM purchased Hughes Aircraft, and it was his interest in opera that took me onto the board of directors of Opera Pacific in Orange County. After retiring from GM, Don became assistant secretary of defense under Dick Cheney. Now he was consulting with Hughes Electronics, principally working with Mike Armstrong.

Overseeing Delco Santa Barbara, I was confronted early on with a rather difficult decision related to their emerging "carousel" inertial sensor. Its origins go back to Don Atwood years before this time. Sparing you the analysis, it became apparent to me that we would not be successful pursuing the device into the commercial aircraft market, which was now dominated by Litton Industries. Before making the decision to terminate the product, I called Don for his opinion. After I had walked him through the facts as I saw them, he said, "If what you say is true, I think you should close it down." I said, "Yes, but what I'm really asking you is whether you think my stated facts are indeed true." Perhaps he had gotten too far away from the market or perhaps he just didn't want to have to vote on terminating the "carousel" inertial sensor he had originated. I don't know. He didn't offer me any further advice on the subject, leaving it to me.

I shut down the emerging product line and had to write off $30 million of development costs that Delco had inventoried. This would have kept us from making our target for the year. Fortunately, at the same time, we were able to change over their accounting procedures to Hughes systems procedures, which gave us a one-time profit windfall, also around $30 million. Three years later, the rest of the inertial sensors product line was sold to Litton Industries.

GM Canada was building lightweight, rubber-tired tanks, with the turrets being shipped to Delco Santa Barbara to be outfitted with Hughes laser rangefinders and fire control systems as well as other equipment. The turrets were then shipped back to Canada for integration into the tank. The cost of the turret with our installed components came to about half the cost of the entire tank. Because the content supplied by our sector was a significant portion of the overall cost of the tank, GM wanted us to take over the business. GM Canada would then supply the chassis to us as a subcontactor.

I was never taken with the idea, but, nevertheless, I took a trip to London, Canada, to look things over. Before I left Mike Armstrong asked me why I was going to Canada. I casually responded, "Oh, to buy a tank factory." I enjoyed the trip and learned a lot about tanks and also their principal business, diesel train locomotives, built in the same factory. After I returned Mike asked, "How did it go?" I just said, "I'm not going to buy a tank factory." The subject never came up again with Mike.

After Operation Desert Storm, the Saudis started buying military planes and what-have-you from the U.S. and the UK. They wanted to purchase a particular British tank which, once again, had a sizable fraction of its cost going to Delco Santa Barbara. Surprisingly, I learned the Saudis were running cash poor, and the British were offering to carry the costs, thereby keeping the English tank factory open. A Parliament member from Scotland raised an objection when he learned a significant portion of the UK funds were really going to the U.S.; that is, to Delco Santa Barbara.

Realizing some of the electronics could be manufactured at Hughes Microelectronics Limited in Scotland, I called Ian Duffin, the general manager of the subsidiary, and told him to meet me in Birmingham; I could get him some business. As a result, a fair portion of the UK investment went to Scotland rather than the U.S., and the Scottish parliamentarian dropped his objections. What else from my trip to Birmingham? Oh, yes: Driving one of their medium-weight tanks around the test track in Birmingham, I almost wiped out a fence, forgetting there is a lot of tank on the left side of the driver.

COMPETING FOR CAPITAL DOLLARS

Each year the sectors would request corporate approval of their capital investments for the following year. Making what I thought was a brilliant, forceful presentation for $80 million for the Aerospace and Defense Sector, I succeeded in getting about $75 million.

Next on the agenda that day was Tony Iorillo, who was ready to build and launch the first DirecTV satellite. For that, he needed $200 million plus another $200 million for a second bird to be left on the ground as a backup. Then he asked for yet another $100 million. "What is that for?" Armstrong wanted to know. "Oh, just in case we need it," he said. Well, Tony got his $500 million.

Afterwards I commented to Tony, "Your slush fund is larger than my entire request!" The $500 million was well spent. Of all the successes at Hughes in replacing military electronics with commercial business, DirecTV is the winner.

USO CELEBRATION

In recognition of the contributions made by the USO (the real name is United Services Organization) during the first Gulf War, a delightful affair was held at Universal Studios. At least 500 people enjoyed a delicious lunch under a humongous tent. There seemed to be more celebrities present than for an Academy Awards ceremony. Three ex-presidents, President Ford, President Reagan, and the first President Bush, were in attendance. Depending on the contribution, you could have your picture taken with Colin Powell, Dick Cheney, or Reagan. Hughes had paid the top amount, enabling Cassie and me to have our picture taken with President and Nancy Reagan.

Following the luncheon, the crowd went to a large studio for a two-hour production scheduled for television viewing at a later date. Bob Hope was one of the masters of ceremonies. He and his wife got lost on the way to the studio, so Cassie and I led them over.

CHAPTER FIVE: 1994–1997

AUTOMOTIVE ELECTRONICS

ACQUISITIONS, MERGERS, AND STRATEGIC PARTNERSHIPS

By 1994 acquisitions, mergers, and reorganizations were rampant throughout military electronics, automotive electronics, and satellite communications companies. In general the transaction decisions were above my level of responsibility, yet I was involved in a number of the fits and starts and eventually was caught up in changes underway that made my career at Hughes take a whole new turn.

An early example of my involvement in inter-company activities was when CEO Mike Armstrong asked me to be a point of contact between Hughes and IBM. I took on the task while helping to run the Aerospace and Defense Sector with Brandes. Mike came to Hughes from IBM, where he had been on the short list to head the company and left to join Hughes when they picked Louis Gerstner, an outsider, as CEO. Well, as you might imagine, just keeping up with Mike, who continued to maintain his multiple contacts at IBM, was difficult, and in fact nearly impossible. It was clear to me, however, that Gerstner was intent on keeping an eye on just what Mike might be up to with his contacts within IBM. Nevertheless, I did pull off a few small items, and Mike and I got to know each other a little better.

In the early days, Hewlett-Packard (HP) and Hughes Aircraft had a number of management similarities and would share ideas on management styles. In addition Hughes was a purchaser of HP products; I seem to remember it was on the order of $50 million per year in the mid-'80s. At Fullerton we teamed with HP for a major U.S. government contract for laptop computers, but somewhere along the line, HP broke rank with us, which led to some heated corporate-level discussions. We got it worked out, but by then Mike Armstrong had appointed me to another corporate-to-corporate responsibility for strategic partnerships. The assignment was about the same as with IBM, but this time I had more elbow room to work.

Texas Instruments (TI) was a major supplier of semiconductors and products using semiconductors. In addition, they had a military weapons operation, though not nearly as large as ours. Our company undertook an initiative to explore the acquisition of TI's military operations. Dick Brandes and I flew down to Dallas to look it over. This was my first experience in a possible acquisition of this magnitude. It came to naught, however. If I remember correctly, there was a minor merger in an area where Dick had the lead. Still it was a good learning experience for me.

Finally, a major acquisition opportunity came up when IBM decided to sell their entire Federal Systems business, with major facilities in upstate New York and around Washington D.C. Under Mike Armstrong's leadership, we attended a series of presentations in New York arranged by one of the major investment banks and took a trip to Federal Systems headquarters in Binghamton, New York. I wondered if I might be asked to oversee operations and perhaps have to relocate to New York. Pure speculation on my part of a possibility that probably would have never come up, but I did ponder whether I would be prepared to make such a move. I'll skip over the ins and outs of this major acquisition, which had some interesting intrigue better left to the principals. The acquisition by Hughes never got that far along before another company made a preemptive purchase, ending the acquisition discussions.

And now, closer to the topic of this chapter, Hughes Electronics' relationship with its parent company was starting to be open for discussion. Had the simple acquisition of Hughes Aircraft in 1985 outlived its purpose, or should it be redefined? What was the value of Hughes to the parent company, as GM was struggling to make ends meet? Note: GM's purchase of Ross Perot's Electronic Data Systems (EDS) in the 1980s was dissolved for reasons unique to GM and EDS. I don't care to discuss any of the details of the ideas that came forth, but I became fairly intimate with the relationships of Hughes, Delco Electronics, and GM's corporate office.

ANOTHER NEW ASSIGNMENT

My increasing involvement with Delco and GM led to a meeting that I had not anticipated. Without warning, Mike Armstrong called me into his office. It was 1994. He asked when I was going to retire. Not at all sure where this conversation was going, I said, "I am 59 and plan to stay on until I am 65 in 2000." He paused and then said, "Good. I just wanted to be sure you had enough runway left for the assignment. There is no one in the corporate office that is from Delco

Electronics or is worrying for them. I want you to be me for Delco Electronics." It was located in Indiana. I took the job on the spot, fully recognizing I would be working with automotive electronics instead of military electronics and that this would be a full-time assignment.

The official announcement stated I was to be the Hughes Aircraft executive for General Motors, reporting to Mike to coordinate all Hughes activities in the automotive market. I was to have all the electric vehicle activities of Hughes and Delco reporting to me. In addition I was placed on Delco's executive staff and retained my position as a member of the Office of the Chairman.

The truth of the matter is Mike didn't elaborate on what he expected from me, but later I told him how I described the task: "GMH has released 400 million shares of stock. If we can get Delco and Hughes working together successfully, the market will take note. For every one dollar increase in equity that the market perceives, I will be adding $400 million to the value of GM Hughes." He liked my definition of the job, and we never again discussed the nature of the assignment; I just sorted it out as we went along.

So, after 32 years in military electronics, I exchanged my job for one in automotive electronics at a drop of a hat. In some ways I was apprehensive, as this would definitely be broken-field running with rather ill-defined responsibilities, yet I was excited about taking on something new.

My immediate task was learning just what was underway between Hughes and Delco and how I could contribute. There were a number of ongoing activities, mostly of a minor nature except for the big one, the EV-1 electric car.

GM's ELECTRIC VEHICLE, THE EV-1

Several of the major automobile companies around the world were undertaking the development of various types of alternative engine vehicles. In the 1990s GM was clearly the leader with the EV-1, a pure electric first-generation vehicle intended to reach at first a limited market in California and Arizona. It carried 1,000 pounds of lead-acid batteries and would go about 70 miles before charging would be necessary.

California's early-'90s mandate that 5 percent of new automobiles be zero-emission vehicles by the year 2000 was the driver behind the effort. I doubt anyone really believed the mandate would be met, yet it spurred GM to take a lead in new alternative automotive systems.

GM Delphi had a division in Indianapolis that provided the battery system and other elements of the EV-1 program. We formed a joint subsidiary to integrate contributions of Delphi, Delco, and Hughes. A new facility was built on Hague Road in Indianapolis for administration and final integration.

MAGNA-CHARGE FOR THE EV-1

The Electron Dynamics Division (EDD) at IEG played a significant role on the EV-1 by providing the battery charging system and in-vehicle power conversion electronics. The operation was pulled out of EDD and reported to me. The charging system, called Magna-Charge, employed an induction paddle that the operator would insert into the car to charge the batteries. Using induction charging without metal contacts, one could plug the charger into the car and provide high charging currents without fear of electrocution, even while standing in rainwater. In turn, this enabled us to build very high-wattage charging stations, which directly reduced the time required to recharge the batteries. Our standard Magna-Charge system drew three kilowatts. We had a prototype 25-kilowatts systems and a 50-kilowatt system in preliminary design. These higher-current systems would eventually be installed by the electric companies, probably at conventional gas stations. We gave Southern Edison a license to take the lead in both California and Arizona for the installation of the charger stations, which they did at some locations, such as Fry's Electronics. I had one in my garage.

At the time, Ford was the other major U.S. automobile company pursuing electric automobiles. However, they chose to just use standard 110 volts for charging the batteries. This meant a full charge would take all night. It was clear to me that if the electric vehicle was to become ubiquitous, essentially replacing internal combustion engines, charging must take place in minutes, not hours. This required lots of power, which would be unacceptably dangerous to handle if metal contacts were used. Over time high-power charging stations would have to be developed to make pure electric cars available 24-7. And finally, the whole industry would be best served if only one charging system became standard.

Since Hughes had the lead on the charger system for GM, I called the appropriate fellow at Ford to discuss the best charging system for electric cars. Could we agree on a common charging system? With a power engineer expert with me, I showed up in Ford country. We had a good, honest discussion but reached no useful conclusions. In my opinion Ford was treating the California zero-emission requirement rather lightly, so the ultimate charging system was of little concern to them in the '90s, whereas GM and I were more seriously pursuing the task of eventually making electric automobiles practical.

On the other hand, Toyota accepted my invitation to talk about charging systems. We made a deal: $2 million for a paid-up license for our inductive charging system. There was some criticism inside Hughes that I had given it away too cheaply. My argument was that if GM and Toyota joined together, the rest of the industry would have to follow. I encouraged them to use the term Magna-Charge, as we were, so there would be no confusion for the drivers. I'm not aware they ever put the induction charger into service in Japan or elsewhere, as the momentum for pure electric vehicles died down in favor of hybrid systems. And it is only now, some fifteen years later, that pure electric systems are just starting to show up on the market. I know of only one car company using induction charging, which means the rest are either hybrids getting electrical energy from gasoline or are "all-night" chargers using 110-volt low power.

In the fall of 1994, Virginia Power Company held a conference on electric vehicles, at which I gave an invited talk on the subject. Appendix C is my presentation on making electric vehicles a reality.

DRIVING A PROTOTYPE EV-1

Before GM put the EV-1 out for lease by consumers, a number of prototypes were built and distributed to insiders, including one I kept at home. I had two additional Magnachargers installed in the parking garage at corporate. So in 1995, I was driving the 45 miles to corporate, recharging the car at work, and then driving it back home in the evenings. I tried along with GM to get diamond-lane privileges for single passengers in electric vehicles, but it was later before California allowed a limited number of pure electric vehicles to use the lane.

The two-seater was really a lot of fun. I remember Cassie and I taking the car to a restaurant for a New Year's Eve affair. A friend saw us in our EV-1 driving home with our paper hats on, still blowing our noisemakers. Guess we sort of stood out after midnight going along PCH (Pacific Coast Highway) in Newport Beach.

Unlike combustion engines, which need to rev up to high speeds before reaching maximum torque, an electric motor has its maximum torque when it first rotates. This means I could out-drag a Mercedes sports car from a stoplight. Newport Beach has a lot of Mercedes sports cars, and I couldn't resist out-dragging them to that next stoplight. Of course, after about 30 miles an hour, the Mercedes could easily zip by. Also, my battery charge indicator would show I really paid a penalty in miles left on the battery.

Eventually GM introduced the EV-1 in California and Arizona with two-year leases for some number vehicles, probably less than a thousand, and then abruptly ended the project. A retired Hughes executive who had helped in the early work had one of the leased cars. GM almost had to drag it away from him, he loved it so. A book has been written on the introduction of the EV-1 and its subsequent withdrawal from the market, a withdrawal which arguably was a strategic mistake.

Most Delco and Hughes people assumed I was associated with Delco only because of the EV-1. Well, yes, it certainly was a major task, but the EV-1 project was only one element of the Hughes/Delco relation. My job was to get Delco and Hughes working together across the board on products and innovations. Gary Dickinson, the president of Delco Electronics, was also a member of the Office of the Chairman and appreciated my efforts towards the two shops working together. Typically I was spending a week at Delco in Kokomo, Indiana, and then a week back in southern California.

In the summer of 1995, the chief technical director at Delco was slated to move to Detroit to head engineering for the luxury car segment, and Gary Dickinson would need a replacement. I could see that Gary might ask me to take this position within Delco. Although it would not be completely necessary, I felt if I accepted an offer, we should move to Indiana. I brought the possibility up with Cassie... would she be prepared to leave Newport Beach and move to Indiana?

She said she would, and I left the subject there.

CHIEF TECHNICAL OFFICER, DELCO ELECTRONICS

That fall, when Gary Dickinson and I were in old historic Kyoto, Japan, following a sales meeting earlier that week in Tokyo, we made a deal. I would come on board as chief technical officer while retaining my other positions as senior corporate vice president and member of the Office of the Chairman. In other words, I would have two jobs: working for Gary in Kokomo, Indiana, on advanced products, while in parallel reporting to our common boss, Mike Armstrong. A little tricky, but Gary, Mike, and I made it work. While in Japan, after agreeing to this arrangement, we enjoyed a lively sushi dinner along with some of the other Delco employees.

Cassie and I found a beautiful home in a gated community on Geist Reservoir north of Indianapolis while keeping our Balboa Peninsula Point home in Newport Beach. I checked out of my office at corporate but had a visitor's office I would use when in town.

As chief technical officer at Delco, one of my principal responsibilities was to provide senior management over the Advanced Technology Center, led by a very talented manager, Dr. Bob Schumacher, who had transferred earlier to Delco from Hughes Research Labs in Malibu. Before I was a significant contributor, the technical center pulled off a significant event by stuffing a custom version of a Chevrolet S-10 with a wide assortment of advanced features. This SSC (Safety, Security, and Communication) concept car was a highlight of the January auto show in Detroit with car features five and ten years ahead of its time. Today, many of these features are now common in cars. The extensive list of advanced technology features included for safety: forward and rear collision warning, adaptive cruise control, night vision, high-intensity discharge lighting, front and side airbags, occupant sensing, and low tire-pressure warning; for security: keyless entry, keyless ignition, electronic lock and latch, intrusion sensing, anti-car jack system, mayday, and perimeter lighting; and for communication: telepath, hands-free cellular, roadside to vehicle communications, 200-watt audio system, data paging, and color reconfigurable displays.

Delco built two of these safety, security, and communication cars for trade shows. Later one of them was donated to Disney and was put on display at Disneyland in the Technology of Tomorrow building.

In addition to the Advanced Technology Center, I had P&L responsibility for Delco's semiconductor operations. Delco semiconductors just happened to be the largest semiconductor supplier in the United States after IBM that sold principally to their own parent company. GM used a lot of semiconductors and solid-state sensors. Motorola was the other principal supplier to GM. Although on a vastly larger scale, the responsibility sure brought me back to those days in Newport Beach, some ten years or so before, when I last had semiconductor responsibility.

Now that GM was no longer favoring their internal component suppliers, Delco's semiconductor operations had to be more competitive in their pricing and needed to expand their limited external sales. These two tasks became the focus of my contribution, leaving the semiconductor technology to the experts in the operation.

Before I arrived, Gary had moved some of our software development to India. Now software technology operations fell under my responsibility. At the end of the first year of our using India, I was not happy with the results, and neither were most of Delco's product engineers. We had to redo much of their work with little to no net savings. Since Gary wanted to keep trying to off-load to India, for the second year I arranged for a rotation of two Indian software engineers to Kokomo every three months to improve coordination with our product engineers. And I kept sending Christy, my director for software technology, over to India. After all, we not only wanted to cut costs, but we had to perform on schedule. Adding it all up, I believe offloading software development to India was at that time, and still is (from what I can observe) simply a bad idea.

GM was still in the grips of EDS's handling all its software and computer services, including Delco. This was a colossal mistake that GM eventually turned around. Delco's chief information officer (CIO) for information systems also reported to me and was stuck with having to work exclusively with EDS. EDS booked about $100 million with Delco per year working through our CIO.

EDS had bad habits, such as telling us what computers we could have and when we could have them. On one occasion, they refused to purchase some computers we wanted until a later date in order to get a better price. When we did get the computers, they didn't pass the savings on to us, just kept it for themselves. However, it wasn't long before they learned I wouldn't put up with all of this nonsense. My favorite example: EDS specified the cell phones for all the Delco executives, which currently were phones that resembled a brick—in fairness perhaps the standard for the times. After Motorola's senior vice president for cellular phones showed me the first of their forthcoming small flip-top cell phones, I requested one, but EDS said I couldn't have it. I reminded the EDS manager that I was responsible for advanced electronics for automobiles and asked him if they were suggesting they would not allow me to become familiar with advanced cell phones? Very shortly thereafter, the rest of the Delco executives all wanted to know how I got a flip-top through EDS.

However, what goes around comes around. Cassie saw my flip-top phone and wanted one, also. When they came on the open market, I paid $1,000 for hers.

INDIANAPOLIS 500 RACE

Gary Dickinson really supported the Indianapolis 500 Memorial Day race and was underwriting race cars. One year Delco was the main sponsor of the Saturday Indy 500 parade. At the Queen's Ball dinner that year, we hosted the VIP guest for the race, Regis Philbin. Cassie seemed to really enjoy the evening.

At the track Delco had a suite on the infield right after turn four, where we could host maybe 200 people for the race. Jim Nabors always opened the race by singing "Back Home Again in Indiana" just before the famous announcement, "Ladies and Gentlemen, start your engines." When Jim visited the Delco suite during the race, Cassie told him he was probably the only person who knew all the words to the song.

On behalf of Delco, I accepted the Louis Schwitzer Award for the best technology innovation being developed for the Indy 500 in 1996. The Advanced Technical Center had designed a helmet-mounted display that enabled the race driver to monitor gauges without glancing down. This is significant when you note that an Indy car can travel 320 feet in one second. If I remember correctly, the key gauge was manifold pressure. You want to keep right at but not over a certain pressure, particularly during time trials for starting positions. Because of the Schwitzer award, during the week of the Indy 500, I was interviewed by ESPN in the garage area standing with the helmet next to our Delco race car. It was televised by ESPN so many times that week, a friend in California said he would turn off the TV if he saw me one more time.

Incidentally, a key technology of the helmet display came from Hughes. In general a number of opportunities for Hughes to contribute to GM were identified, whether going through Delco or to GM directly. Bob Kurkjian, who reported to me at that time, played a valuable role in linking Hughes in general and the Malibu Research Center in particular to GM. He was also very helpful in linking me to key managers within GM, as he knew almost everyone. Bob is the brother of Lou, with whom I worked closely at Ground Systems in Fullerton.

CONVERGENCE 1996

Each year there was a conference titled Convergence that addressed the convergence of the electronics industry with the automobile industry. The general idea of convergence of these two was already a well-accepted fact by the 1990s, but it provided a good opportunity for the electronics firms, such as Delco, to show their wares.

I was asked to chair an afternoon session on the emerging opportunities for GPS for automobiles. Nothing was yet available for automobiles, and the U.S. government was still deliberately blurring the location information for commercial applications, protecting high accuracy for the military. It was a lot of fun hearing the various speakers give their visions of the use of GPS in automobiles, but I must admit I missed just how extensive the navigation applications would become. I had already driven a car with an early "turn-here" guidance system, but I seriously underestimated just how much directional information could be stored economically. For example, I commented companies such as McDonald's might give away CDs with information on how to find one of their stores. Not a particularly bad idea, except that information plus just about everything else you would like to know are already installed in your GPS device today essentially for free.

INTERFACING WITH GM CORPORATE

Before getting into my experiences with GM, I will digress for a moment. Over the years, GM was always high in my consciousness. As a child I learned to drive in the family Buick and eventually married a woman who was driving a Buick. In the late '40s, with the guiding hand of Grandpa Scott, I took the money I earned selling peanuts at the baseball games in my hometown of Statesville, North Carolina, and bought two shares of GM, my first stock purchase. In 1964 I sold the GM stock, which had multiplied through stock splits, to help purchase our first home in Canoga Park. We sold that home to buy our second home, Homewood, in 1973. When we sold Homewood, the funds were used to purchase our home in Newport Beach. Recently, the Newport Beach house sold, and the peanut-earnings–to-GM-stock-to-real-estate-capital assets are now in the equity of our apartment in Hawaii, where it will sit awhile. In summary, when the Howard Hughes Medical Institute put Hughes Aircraft up for sale in 1985, I wanted GM to win the bidding over Ford Motor Company, and they did.

Now to various incidental experiences I had with General Motors.

1992 BOARDROOM COUP

Roger Smith, who was CEO when GM bought Hughes Aircraft, retired in 1990 and was replaced by Bob Stempel, an engineer by trade who was well liked by the technical community. However, in 1992, as the fortunes of GM continued to decline, a key outside director of GM saw that it was time for another change in leadership.

As they did from time to time, the GM board of directors met at Hughes headquarters in California. On this particular occasion, there was a luncheon in the Hughes executive dining room, after which I was to make a short presentation to the board. Bob Stempel and various Hughes and GM executives sat at the head table. I was seated at a small side table with three external members of the board. During lunch, it wasn't long before I realized the retired CEO and chairman of Proctor and Gamble, and now a key external member of the GM board, was not at my table with two other outside board members only to have lunch. He was busy signing them up for a vote of no confidence and the removal of Bob Stempel as CEO. When he apologized for not including me in routine luncheon talk, I simply nodded an acknowledgement. The board cancelled the Hughes presentations that afternoon and voted Bob out. They gave the job of CEO to Jack Smith. Jack was selected after passing over Lloyd Reuss, the president of General Motors and heir apparent. That was a rather interesting lunch, witnessing a boardroom coup.

After Jack Smith had been named CEO, Reuss, an engineer by trade, was sitting at my table during dinner. Jack dropped for a cordial hello. In truth, not really knowing, I asked, "Are you engineering or finance?" He said, "Finance." I retorted, "Shucks. I was hoping you were an engineer." Boy, did that get a good therapeutic laugh out of Lloyd Reuss. He had been passed over for the job as the board wanted to transfer from engineering to financial leadership.

Both Reuss and Stempel retired shortly thereafter. As I'm writing this in 2010, it may be worth mentioning that last December, Mark Reuss, Lloyd's son, was named president of GM North American operations in the "new" GM. He is an engineer.

Shortly after Bob Stempel left office, I visited him in his small office in the Detroit area, seeking advice on energy storage technology for electric vehicles. His past secretary was still working for him. I asked why he had such a long conference desk in his small office. Bob said GM had asked him to work various customer vehicle claims, and it took a lot of lawyers.

We had several other opportunities to be together, and we always enjoyed each other's company.

ALTERNATIVE PROPULSION SYSTEMS

I never completely made peace with being held down to the role Delco was given to play as a sub-subcontractor. Given the opportunity, I welcomed dialog at higher levels, such as one I had with Jack Smith regarding electric vehicles and other alternatives to internal combustion engines. We shared the same opinion that pure electric was only one approach to alternative propulsion systems, and that we should explore a wide range of possibilities including hybrids, fuel cells, and advanced diesel.

GM had all the advanced technologies it needed, but just wouldn't let them blossom. For example, I had driven a Delphi hybrid vehicle at a time Toyota was not yet close to bringing out their Prius hybrid, yet GM allowed itself to fall behind. Admittedly, I am just a neophyte in the complicated, multidimensional automotive world and should defer to good people with better insight, but it needed to let good people be heard; the company was just too insular to change.

MIGHT MAKES RIGHT

At Hughes I always felt the management style was such that "Right Makes Might." As a middle manager at Hughes, I argued once all the way up to the president of the company that my version of what to do in one particular situation was right, with the intermediate managers just standing back out of the way, letting me make my argument. However, I sensed that at GM "Might Makes Right" predominated while I was there.

I sat in at a high-level GM monthly management meeting once representing Mike Armstrong. Mike was a member of the top-level management committee but couldn't be there for some reason. We had a non-controversial message to present, and he gave me the task. Sitting around a table with the top GM executives, it struck me there just wasn't enough openness in their various discussions. I provided my message and stayed quiet as expected; this was not my turf. At an equivalent Hughes Office of the Chairman meeting, I would not have hesitated to speak up, whether controversial or not.

The "might" at GM extended to control of its external members of the board of directors; that is, before the board revolt in 1992 I have already described. As a good example, I was sent to New York to prepare Don Atwood, vice chairman of GM, to present a request from Hughes to the board to purchase a company in Canada for $80 million. That I didn't think this was a good idea was not the point, because my CEO at Hughes wanted to buy the company. So over a delightful dinner with Don at the Plaza Hotel, I gave him the details of our request. He was fast to understand the economics of the proposal. Because I could see there were other ways to proceed to meet our objective other than buying a company, I asked, "Don't you need to offer the board alternatives?" He said, "No, we just tell them this is what we want." In passing, we got the money, but on the company plane back to L.A., I was pleased to learn another company had already offered more than our $80 million and that ended this venture.

SCIENTIFIC ADVISORY BOARD

On several occasions Delco was visited by the General Motors Board of Directors' Science Advisory Board, a rather august group with six members. Now here was an environment in which I could express myself openly. After all, what is the purpose of such an advisory board if not to see further into the future? I argued that GM needed to elevate the electronics in their vehicles to a higher level in the organization. Historically automotive electronics have expanded in small increments, starting first with radios. Today a car is increasingly under the control of electronics, while the design of the electronics are still held down as a low sub-tier component. Obviously, bringing electronics all the way up to almost first tier would "break a lot of crystal," and the well-established lead organizations would lose a measure of importance and control. Yet today, a car can be characterized by its electronics just as well as by other attributes. Dr. Robert Solow, a Nobel laureate in economics and head of the Science Advisory Board, understood my observation but said, "Scott, I don't see one centillionth of evidence that GM is thinking this way." My answer, "That is exactly my point." Perhaps today, almost fifteen years later, to some extent some of this vision is starting to happen in the "new GM."

PRESENTATIONS TO NEW GM EXECUTIVES

Frequently I was asked to give a talk about GM Hughes to GM managers who had arrived at some level or other of higher management. They would spend a week in Detroit getting briefings on all the operations that make up GM worldwide. GM Hughes was always scheduled to be the final topic on Friday, and I treated my talk like their dessert, as none of them were likely to ever work at GM Hughes. On occasion I would show up a day or so early to sit in on presentations by other GM senior managers. A highlight would be the Thursday evening tour of the design studio, seeing future generations of autos in full-size clay.

I had fun commenting, "You might think Hughes goes around GM like the planet Earth goes around the sun. Well, let me remind you, the Earth does not go around the sun. The Earth and the sun go around their common center of gravity. It's true that this center of gravity is only 100 miles from the center of the sun." They got it. The presenters were always sent a report card provided by each of the new executives stating what they thought of your presentation. I kept batting 100. A typical comment might be something like, "Wish we could operate like Hughes," which was exactly what I was trying to get across.

DRESS CODES IN CORPORATE AMERICA

Still, in their own way, GM was trying to break away from out-dated behavior patterns, just like IBM was trying to do. To illustrate with a simple example, I joined Mike Armstrong on the company Gulfstream for two meetings. The first meeting was in Detroit with Jack Smith, GM's CEO, and then on to IBM on the East Coast for a meeting with Lou Gerstner, the successful new CEO of IBM. Meetings with the heads of two of the nation's largest companies were without coat and tie; in fact traditional business attire would have been out of place, since they wanted to force changes in their employees' habits.

Another little example… Jack had his top GM executives wear their watches on their right arms until they got things turned around. A year or so later, I noticed he was wearing his watch on his left wrist and commented that GM must be making money again. Yes, times were changing.

THE WRAP UP

Referring to the French Revolution, Charles Dickens wrote, "It was the best of times, it was the worst of times." Perhaps that also describes GM Hughes in the mid-'90s. The Cold War that defined much of my career at Hughes was over. We had won. The world agreed on a western capitalistic style of society. Technology was driving the economy, with vastly expanded communication systems at the fore-front. Second-tier world countries were achieving their place at the head tables, and third-world countries aspired to join them. Life ex-pectancy was increasing, both in longevity and in daily existence. The totally unnecessary radical beliefs that are disrupting the world's society today had not yet become front and center.

Yet in these times, GM Hughes was undergoing a tsunami that tore it apart. Setting aside the aircraft industry, Hughes had been once the largest military electronics company in the world. When we merged with General Motors, we became an adjunct to the world's largest employer. And now all of this was changing.

Delco, which once had about 23 percent of the world market for automobile electronics, could no longer provide the profits it once did. The military industry was consolidating, eliminating company after company. Arguably Hughes Electronics could have survived as a boutique electronics company, but now we were a Wall Street commodity, and that would not be an option. We needed to merge with someone. It turned out to be Raytheon, which came hard for those of us who had spent most of our lives competing with this company

And worse, our parent company, General Motors, was spiraling irretrievably into what fifteen years later would become a bankruptcy and being saved from extinction by a government bailout. But that was the future. In the mid-1990s, it was simply time to sell off assets to keep GM alive, which included things like the GM corporate building in New York, and more to the point at this moment, GM Hughes.

First GM sold all of our military weapons and systems operations to Raytheon. They extracted Delco, a $5.5 billion operation, from Hughes, merged it with Delphi, a $30 billion operation, and spun it all off. (They also ended up in bankruptcy and are only now trying to come back. I think they will.) The other pieces of Hughes were also sold off, with the purchase by Boeing of our satellite operation being most noteworthy. When GM was through, they had received about $15 billion for all of the pieces.

The biggest remaining operation was DirecTV, a Hughes innovation that defined TV distribution to homes using transmission from Hughes-invented synchronous orbit satellites. DirectTV went public, with the major owner being Rupert Murdoch, followed later by John Malone. The company is the leading alternative to ground-based cable television and is profitable.

So where do I and my career all fit in? As a youngster I might have spotted a golden opportunity in this dispersal of assets. But I was 62, just three years shy of mandatory retirement at age 65. In a different way, this was fortunate in that I could retire a little early without any significant financial loss and simply enjoy an additional three years of retirement living, which is exactly what I did. Not that I had a lot of alternatives, as none of the broken-apart pieces matched my ability to contribute, particularly with so little runway left from which to first taxi and then take off.

So, not all at once or necessarily in this order, the following events eventually happened: Gary Dickerson retired, and Mike Burns, a very capable GM guy, came in to turn things around at Delco. Delco was pulled out of Hughes Electronics, merged with Delphi, and then spun off from GM, so my job working the Hughes/Delco relationship was long gone. My old Aerospace and Defense Sector was sold to Raytheon Corporation. Dick Brandes retired.

Mike Armstrong held a lovely retirement party for me at a private club in west L.A. owned by Murdoch. At the retirement dinner, rather than the traditional statements by my co-workers, he invited my three sons and my wife to speak. I was proud almost to the point of tears as Tyler, Morgan, and Brandon separately spoke about their father. Cassie, bless her soul, chose to say, "Mike, thank you for making us rich." Oh dear, a clear overstatement. Armstrong also left within the year.

Retiring at age 62, I quickly fell into a whole new life. I turned down three offers to consult, and then the offers stopped coming in. I pleasantly surprised myself that I could let go of Hughes so easily. I still keep up contacts and particularly enjoy being with my old co-workers from IEG at our annual "no-business" offsite meetings.

We've kept our residence in Indianapolis, enjoying boating, croquet, and summer fun when the family gets together. Son Morgan with his wife and three children moved from Hawaii to live down the lake from us.

A few years after retiring, we purchased an apartment in Honolulu as a third home. As I write this report in 2010, we sold the Newport home and expanded our oceanfront residence in Honolulu by purchasing an adjacent apartment. Now we live in Hawaii about half time, and maybe some day full time. In general, we've kept life very simple.

At my retirement dinner, Mike Armstrong said, "Scott, you will be starting a new chapter in your life." I said, "No, I will be starting a whole new book." And I'm busy today living in the new book. The family has grown to fifteen, with Cassie and me the youngest.

But thanks for giving me the opportunity to tell you things As I Remember, the first book.

APPENDIX

I

THE FORMATION OF HUGHES AIRCRAFT COMPANY

Howard Hughes, Jr., was in the first half of the twentieth century one of the wealthiest persons in the world. His wealth came from his father, who invented a drilling bit or tool to cut through granite to reach the oil beneath. When his father died, Howard Jr. was in his late teens and through clever maneuvering became the sole owner of the Hughes Tool Company. Before long Hughes moved from Texas to southern California to pursue his interests in aviation and movie making. In 1932 he formed the Hughes Aircraft Company within the parent Hughes Tool Company to further his interests in airplanes. His exploits became world famous and included setting airplane speed records, records for flying around the world, and making films

During World War II, Hughes Aircraft Company (often abbreviated as HAC) developed the Flying Boat as a means to circumvent the sinking of our ships by German submarines, although the war ended before this record-breaking airplane was completed. Nevertheless, as the war ended, Hughes had to decide what to do with HAC and directed the small engineering company towards military electronics, particularly missiles, radar, and infrared sensors.

When the Soviet Union developed nuclear weapons, the United States had a serious problem: how to defend itself against incoming Soviet bombers carrying nuclear bombs. Hughes Aircraft succeeded with the design of a series of Falcon air-to-air missiles and the associated radars, infrared sensors, and avionics. As a result, HAC became a critical military supplier to the U.S. Air Force.

Hughes developed a reputation as a very wealthy, very eccentric playboy, which largely was deserved. As a consequence, by the early 1950s the government became concerned about their dependence on Hughes to supply key elements of our nation's strategic defense system. In response, in 1953 Hughes decided to spin Hughes Aircraft Company out of Hughes Tool Company and set up the not-for-profit Howard Hughes Medical Institute, which then owned Hughes Aircraft Company. The profits from HAC went to the Medical Institute, which in term distributed funds for medical research to Howard Hughes Medical Fellows at various universities around the country. As a result, until the Bill and Melinda Gates Foundation of recent years, Howard Hughes made the world's largest private donation to medical research.

Hughes hired Pat Hyland as general manager of Hughes Aircraft Company and largely removed himself from operations. From then forward, Hughes had little involvement with Hughes Aircraft Company. As Hughes Aircraft Company grew to become the world's largest military electronics company, insiders rather enjoyed the confusion of the company title misnomers, which essentially had little or nothing to do with Howard Hughes and never produced an aircraft. Since the company was privately owned, it did not matter how Wall Street assessed the company. The elimination of aircraft from the company name finally occurred when General Motors purchased the company in 1985 and it became GM Hughes Electronics. And starting then, as Wall Street began to play its traditional role, it was important not to have a misleading title for the company.

II

KEYNOTE ADDRESS AT UC IRVINE GROUND-BREAKING CEREMONY MAY 7, 1992

FORMING A PARTNERSHIP FOR A COMPLEX WORLD

Good afternoon, Executive Vice Chancellor Smith, Dean Sirignano, and other distinguished faculty and guests. It is a pleasure to participate in this groundbreaking for UCI's new engineering building, which so typifies the dynamic growth of the university. We are indeed witnessing the coming of age of a very fine university. The School of Engineering, in particular, has recently been recognized as one of the top five "up and coming" engineering schools in America. The school now has on the order of 1,000 undergraduate students and 300 graduate students and may well double by the year 2000.

It is a tribute to both UCI and the School of Engineering that the state of California has provided the funds for this expansion. It is a testimony to the contributions you have been making. You are also to be congratulated on improving the quality of the school while you grow.

The university sees as its mission the responsibility to educate our youth, to conduct fundamental research, and to be of public service. To accomplish this mission, the university has formed a three-way partnership that consists of academia, the government, and industry. Today, I will develop some ideas regarding this powerful partnership, which can serve us well by dealing with some very complex problems.

The government has several roles to play, not the least of which is the responsibility to fund long-range research—research with paybacks 5 to 20 years out in the future, or even uncertain in their time frame. This is an essential role for government, as the sizes of fundamental research projects are becoming increasingly outside the realm industry can support. Another job of government is to do the social engineering surrounding the activities our partnership pursues, as well as to carry out the associated regulations.

Industry's job is to take projects to the market and also to meet short-term research requirements, say one to five years.

Academia fuels the system with educated women and men and conducts breakthrough research.

This partnership is a good one that serves us well in a complex, rapidly changing world. One face of this rapidly changing world is aerospace and defense. Our partnership has been very active, but now the (Cold) war, which lasted 45 years, is over.

The gross national product (GNP) dedicated to defense is typically on the order of 10 percent during times of hot wars, such as Korea or Vietnam. The military buildup during the 80's peaked at around 6.5 percent (without any shooting). That has now been reduced to about 4.5 percent and may likely go down to the order of 3.5 percent, which I believe is comparable to the time of the 30's, before World War II. This cutback is having a significant impact on our partnership.

Clearly, it will affect the careers of many government employees, will result in the closing of many military bases and depots, and will reduce funding to governmental laboratories doing applied research. Industry will also have a shakeout. One fallout is the lesser degree to which advanced research will be funded by the military. And also affected, of course, will be the amount of this funding that has been passing through to academe. In addition there will be less demand for scientists and engineers coming from the universities. The defense activities won't just go away, but they will be reduced. The change is having particular impact in southern California, where aerospace and defense have been dominant.

Now this isn't the end of the world; in fact it is the beginning of a new, exciting world, one in which our three-way partnership can address new opportunities. The question can be asked, which industries are robust enough to supplement or replace the aerospace market? This is not a trivial question. The computer industry and the emerging information management industry are growth industries. Bioengineering is another. Space activities should be strong, first with earth observatories and then the colonization of space during the twenty-first century. However, I would like to highlight three industries that are particularly suitable for our partnership.

The first is transportation. Already, the governor has asked a Blue Ribbon Committee to identify means to improve our transportation and at the same time create a new growth industry for California. There are opportunities for high-speed trains, electric vehicles, smart highways, and toll road systems, to name a few. Industry and academe are prepared to meet their obligations for these projects while the government is lagging in being able to provide the needed direction, primarily because of the very difficult social engineering task involved.

A different but related industry for our partnership is alternative sources of energy. We can expect that the preferred form of energy for final distribution will be electricity, in which case, we need better energy storage technology. This time industry and academe are lagging in playing their respective roles. But more fundamental is the fact that we don't really have an ultimate primary source of energy, one that can meet the needs of the next century. Hydroelectric is nearly built out, and we are at the peak of the fossil fuel era. Nuclear fission has stalled for a number of reasons, including safety and waste disposal, and so far the promise of nuclear fusion has not been fulfilled. Academe really must take the lead on this one; we need some breakthrough technologies.

The third market involves the protection of our environment. This is a challenge for our three-way partnership. Government sets the standards and regulates. Industry is ready and willing to deliver environmental products to the markets. Some breakthrough research is also needed. UCI can be noted for one major contribution it has already made—this is the analysis that led to the prediction of an ozone-depletion effect coming from the release of chemicals such as CFC to the atmosphere. We in industry are now busy finding ways to eliminate these polluting chemicals from our products and processes.

All of these problems are complex and involve high technology—and they also call for contending with thorny human behaviors. I would like to ask academe to help better prepare our future leaders to deal with problems of this complex nature. We need the "compleat" engineer, to borrow from Pogo. She or he needs to grasp a wide spectrum of issues at the same time. I encourage more multidisciplinary educational opportunities at the university. They not only help the student get a better perspective, but also can often contribute to breakthroughs by what I call "creativity by analogy." We have all seen it happen, where someone recognizes a solution to a problem by the similarities coming from other fields.

As a corollary, I also have a concern about the closed society in research and publication that locks out new thinking by investigators who come from outside the established cadre of researchers. The establishment can and often does block fresh thinking that runs counter to their views, not unlike the restriction on scientific thought during the dark ages.

On discussing our partnership of academe, government, and industry, I spoke of three market challenges (transportation, alternative energy sources, and environment) where I think we collectively can provide some answers. There is, however, another whole class of challenges, even more complex, for which we haven't yet even formulated a proper course of action.

For example, take social unrest such as we recently saw in Los Angeles. Can we construct a sound approach to generating remedies: can we even articulate the deep-lying roots of the problem? Another such challenge is the economy that has developed around (illicit) drugs. How are we to wipe out this economy? And a third problem, one that has been around at least 5,000 years, is the formulation of religious dogmas that become the basis or at least the rationale for creating considerable turmoil around the world. This seems incredible, recognizing the initial good intents of these religions.

To deal with some of these problems, we need not only leaders, but people with high morality and wisdom. Now, it is perhaps rather difficult to teach wisdom, but may I note you have a course in creative writing—and it would seem equally possible to teach creativity.

You at UCI are to be congratulated on some of your projects, which at least partially address aspects of these rather intangible issues. Your outreach programs to K through 12, particularly your leadership in the minority engineering program, should be noted.

I encourage you to consider more liberal arts education for engineers. The expansion of our continuous education programs should also be a high priority. And let me add, I think the faculty should always be expected to set good examples, as youth learns most easily through examples.

I would like to end by reaching out a little further yet. Someone from industry is often characterized as coming from the "real world." I guess, therefore, that today I'm here in a "non-real world" so perhaps I can dare to let my feet leave the ground a little. I would like to speculate on a new scientific mind, one that goes further than most of us have dared in trying to find solutions to today's very complex problems.

Earlier in this century, we learned to accept the duality of matter. An object can sometimes be best characterized as a particle, and at other times, the object can be best characterized as a wave. Most of us today have learned to accept this duality of matter; it is both a particle and a wave. Perhaps some day someone will show us how this duality can be explained; in the meantime, we have learned to live with a paradox.

Similarly, I would like to suggest that on a much higher level of thought, the scientist/engineer should learn to accept the duality of scientific and spiritual reasoning. There are those who believe we may soon be able to combine the four forces of nature into one explanation, called the theory of everything (TOE). At that time we will have reached a pinnacle of understanding. Well, that may be so, but, as someone has noted, even then we still won't be able to explain something so ordinary as why a dog chases a cat—leave alone understand complex human behavior.

We should just accept this duality of scientific and spiritual reasoning as a paradox until such time as someone can unite the two lines of reasoning. It is like the "right side" and "left side" brain theory. We don't even have common terms for the second half of this duality, but by whatever terms you wish to use, we should accept wisdom or spirituality, or if you will, moral thought, to be just as valid as scientific thought in finding solutions to today's complex problems. Our "compleat" engineer is now asked to be an even broader, multidisciplinary person who can approach a problem from either side.

What is the next step? What should our partnership do next? Given the purpose of today's gathering, that is easy—we should stop and enjoy this blessed moment. Let's stop to celebrate the groundbreaking for a new building, dedicated to education and research—and one that will serve our partnership.

III

MAKING ELECTRIC VEHICLES A REALITY, AN INVITED PAPER AT ELECTRO EXPO, SPONSORED BY VIRGINIA POWER, SEPTEMBER 13, 1994
Rebalancing Energy Sources: Electric Power for Transportation

Thank you, Jim. I am very pleased to have this opportunity to participate in Electro Expo '94. Virginia Power and the other sponsors are to be congratulated for arranging this affair that may prove to be historic. Why? Because a significant event is occurring at the end of this century: we are rebalancing among the alternative sources of energy available for use in transportation. And we are doing so partly by bringing together two large industries, the automotive and the electric utility industries.

There was a similar redistribution among energy sources a century ago when we moved away from horsepower to what eventually settled out to be the internal combustion engine. The main trade-off for transportation energy sources at the beginning of the century was among the internal combustion (or "IC") engine, the steam engine, and the electric motor. The convenience and efficiency of the IC won out over steam, and the efficiency of energy storage in the form of gasoline won out over battery storage for electric motors.

Problems with Petroleum

These trade-offs are still valid today; yet a century later, we're back at it looking for alternatives. There are two reasons. First, the ICs are polluting our atmosphere. Although tremendous gains have been made in reducing emissions, and there are a few things we can still do, the onus is on us to find clean air alternatives. Second, sources of petroleum are dwindling. We are not in danger of depleting these sources in the next 20 or 40 years, but ultimately this will become the problem. Already, however, this reduction in sources of petroleum has led to serious problems with foreign trade balances and a reduction in political stability around the world. The United States, at both federal and state levels, has taken leadership to resolve these two problems with clean air and alternative fuel directives.

Challenges for EVs: Energy Storage and Satisfied IC Users

The most fundamental problem confronting us is finding an efficient form, besides gasoline, in which to store energy for mobile vehicles. In most configurations we like electric motors to generate the mechanical torque; electric motors are very acceptable engines. But whether we end up with pure electric or hybrid EV/IC engines, how do we store the energy? Do we use fuel cells, capacitors, flywheels, or today's choice of batteries? Nevertheless, for most alternatives we will be relying upon the electric utilities to provide the prime energy sources. I believe it is inescapable that our electric utilities will be required to generate and distribute an ever-increasing portion of the energy we use for transportation.

There is a daunting problem, however, that shapes the debate. The IC users (you and I) are personally very satisfied with the IC product. There is not a strong customer pull for EVs. Instead we have collective societal demand for change, not a personal demand. Now, we may argue over how much societal demand there is and how fast it's growing, but I believe it will not go away.

There are a host of infrastructure issues to be resolved: Who pays for a societal demand? How do you rewrite regulator controls to take account of the paradigm shift? What new tax laws should be put in place, and what other incentives should be used?

What Charger to Adopt

Today we are focusing in on yet another issue. What is the electrical equivalent of today's gas station? In particular, we are focusing in on a rather arcane technical issue: How do we configure the charger? How do we couple the utility power to the automobile? Do we conductively couple the two, as we do every day when we plug in a lamp, or do we inductively couple the two? In the latter case, the charger is outside the vehicle, on the utility side. A paddle, which is actually just the primary windings of a transformer, is inserted into the car that contains the secondary windings of the transformer.

From an automotive industry viewpoint we shouldn't really care which coupling technique we use, as long as it is safe, convenient, and low cost. To make electric vehicles happen, we simply want the right technical solution.

Several years ago, GM Hughes Electronics, working with other interested parties, started to address this issue. We reached the conclusion that inductive charging with smart communication between the automobile and the external charger was the correct solution. Now, if this proves to be incorrect, we will abandon the approach. We want to make the electric vehicle a reality, and there is no fundamental reason to hold on to any particular charging technique. However, continued tradeoffs and refinements of alternative charging approaches still strongly favor an inductive solution.

Today we will hear from several people regarding the salient features of inductive charging, but let me emphasize just two. It is the safest for the user and has power qualities and load management issues that have far-reaching implications for the power utilities.

Common Standards a Must: The Best Solution, Whatever It Is

Some progress has been made to resolve or at least clarify questions about the two charging alternatives. In particular, committees have been formed to establish standards, both for conductive and inductive chargers.

Now perhaps that is as far as things will go, and we will again leave it to end users to eventually find a solution for us, or worse, leave them to endure both. It surely brings to mind the struggle between VHS and Betamax video recording formats. However, in that struggle the end objective was to sell a particular video recorder. In this case we only want the best solution, whatever it may be.

Similar instances of senseless alternatives inflicted on society come readily to mind—left- and right-hand drive vehicles, 60- and 50-cycle power, NTSC and PALS TV formats, just to name a few. And yet on occasion we do collectively agree up front, and everyone wins. Consider two examples, both from the music industry. The first is the format for CD audio. We can purchase a CD anywhere on Earth and know it will play in our own machine if arbitrary codes to prohibit it are not in place. Another is the digital format called MIDI for linking musical synthesizers. Equipment from a vast array of suppliers can be controlled using one communication format, something the rest of the computer industry should note with envy.

Utilities Have a Key Role in Building the New Infrastructure

As Jim Rhodes stated earlier this morning, one-third of the nation's energy is consumed for transportation. If we rebalance the equation so that the utility industry is to provide a significant fraction of this transportation energy, there are serious infrastructure issues we must address, not the least of which is the method of transferring this energy to the vehicle.

This is where you from the utilities industries come in. You need to get involved. For your own self interest you need to determine how you can service this major new load while minimizing new investments, and you also need to see how you can help find a solution to a societal demand.

In closing, let me say I think the future is bright for electric vehicles in one form or another. I look forward to the discussions that will occur at Electro Expo '94 with the same interest and excitement I'm sure you have. If we put together a sound infrastructure, we will have taken a significant step towards making electric vehicles a reality.